Blessings,
Cathy Catching

Angel Talk

Angel Talk

A True Story of One Woman's Miraculous Healing
and the Angels Who Got Her Through It

Cathy Catching

BALBOA
PRESS
A DIVISION OF HAY HOUSE

Copyright © 2014 Cathy Catching.

All rights reserved. No part of this book may be used or reproduced by any means, graphic, electronic, or mechanical, including photocopying, recording, taping or by any information storage retrieval system without the written permission of the publisher except in the case of brief quotations embodied in critical articles and reviews.

Balboa Press books may be ordered through booksellers or by contacting:

Balboa Press
A Division of Hay House
1663 Liberty Drive
Bloomington, IN 47403
www.balboapress.com
1 (877) 407-4847

Because of the dynamic nature of the Internet, any web addresses or links contained in this book may have changed since publication and may no longer be valid. The views expressed in this work are solely those of the author and do not necessarily reflect the views of the publisher, and the publisher hereby disclaims any responsibility for them.

The author of this book does not dispense medical advice or prescribe the use of any technique as a form of treatment for physical, emotional, or medical problems without the advice of a physician, either directly or indirectly. The intent of the author is only to offer information of a general nature to help you in your quest for emotional and spiritual well-being. In the event you use any of the information in this book for yourself, which is your constitutional right, the author and the publisher assume no responsibility for your actions.

Any people depicted in stock imagery provided by Thinkstock are models, and such images are being used for illustrative purposes only.
Certain stock imagery © Thinkstock.

Printed in the United States of America.

ISBN: 978-1-4525-2384-2 (sc)
ISBN: 978-1-4525-2386-6 (hc)
ISBN: 978-1-4525-2385-9 (e)

Library of Congress Control Number: 2014918418

Balboa Press rev. date: 11/03/2014

I would like to dedicate this book to God, Jesus, my angels and all of the other heavenly white light beings who made my miracle possible.

Your unwavering love and guidance inspire me to make this world a better place.

Table of Contents

Preface ix

Introduction - Divine Guidance xiii

Chapter 1 - The Early Years 1

Chapter 2 - The Reality of Illness 12

Chapter 3 - A Friend in Need 37

Chapter 4 - Other Methods of Healing 52

Chapter 5 - I Can Hear Angels 72

Chapter 6 - The Miracle 99

Chapter 7 - Road to Recovery 126

Chapter 8 - A Christmas to Remember 149

Chapter 9 - Family of Miracles 167

Chapter 10 - Return to Chimayo..............................196

Epilogue - Angel Talk 211

Appendix A - Legend of Chimayo............................215

Preface

This book tells a story . . . not one of fiction, but of the true account of my miraculous healing and the incredible events surrounding it. Those incredible events began in October, 2011 when I began hearing what I consider the most amazing voices known to man. These voices were musical and uplifting and belonged to none other than God's extraordinary angels!

At the time that I started to hear these amazing voices, I was suffering from a rare and progressive neuromuscular disorder that had rendered me physically disabled. I could no longer work and frequently required the assistance of a cane, walker or motorized scooter for mobility.

The following month, my prayers to God for healing were answered! The progression of my illness abruptly halted and I began to rapidly recover from what is considered an incurable disorder!! With the wonderful help of His angels and other divine beings, I have now made a full recovery!

I am sharing this incredible story to encourage others to believe that all things are possible and to never give up. No matter what your life circumstances are, stay strong in your faith and believe in miracles. We have an amazing supreme being that loves each and every one of us unconditionally. He has also provided many marvelous divine helpers to assist us to be healthy and happy.

I reached out and God, angels and other divine beings were there for me. Their love and guidance healed my mind, body and soul. Angels and other heavenly beings are available for each and every one of us and will communicate, guide and heal us through God. All we have to do is ask.

To my family:
Thank you for your continued love and support.
I am so glad that you are a part of this wonderful journey.

I would also like to thank all of those people who prayed for me during my illness and all of the medical personnel who have tended to me over the years. In particular, I'd like to give special thanks to three doctors who made a difference in my life.

Russell LaForte, M.D.
Robert Smith, M.D., Ph.D.
Owen Bryan Holland, M.D.

Introduction

Divine Guidance

Before I tell you my incredible story, I want you to know that my angels guided me into writing this book and will be inserting messages into every chapter! I sometimes can't distinguish their messages and my thoughts, but it simply doesn't matter.

They are helping me deliver the information that readers need and that is all that counts. Sometimes these messages show up after I wander off topic so be sure and pay particular attention. Although the information may seem unnecessary to some, you can be sure that it will mean something to others.

Some of my wanderings also pertain to personal stories that my angels want me to share. Most of these stories involve divine interaction that I didn't realize was going on at that time. I am sharing these so that you may be able to "see" similar interactions within your own life.

As a matter of fact, I am being "told" that this book will be somewhat interactive for the reader. Pay attention to random thoughts, memories or ideas that "pop" into your head as you read through my story. There may be a message for you within these thoughts so be sure and write them down!

Divine interactions happen all the time and are quite fascinating. I am still amazed at how my angels guided me into becoming clairaudient and subsequently into my miraculous healing! The events that led up to my miracle defy any odds of probability and cannot be explained as simply coincidental.

I am also amazed at the fact that God healed me from a genetic illness. Although it was never officially diagnosed as being genetic, I certainly believe it was. There were too many correlations between my illness and other family members; mainly, my mother and my daughter. Within the first part of this book you will find convincing evidence of that involvement which truly makes my healing supernatural in origin!

And if you are still not quite convinced that all of this is divine in nature, read Chapter Nine. There have been several other healings within our family, including my daughter who had symptoms that paralleled mine! My angels have told me about many of them and that there will be more in the future! This speaks volumes about the power in prayer and divine intervention! So now that your curiosity is piqued, let's get to the meat and potatoes of this book! Don't forget to keep an eye out for those angel messages!

Chapter One

The Early Years

During the first few months after my healing, I spent countless hours reviewing my life. I reflected back to my early years in an attempt to uncover signs of my illness. My goal was to see if I could logically determine whether I had this illness all of my life. It didn't take me much time at all to come to that conclusion.

For as long as I can remember, I experienced some sort of medical problem. As a teenager, I played competitive tennis in school but was always plagued with fatigue issues. I remember being worried that my coaches thought I wasn't trying hard enough. There were times, though, that my body just wouldn't go anymore, particularly when training. I can remember trying to run laps around the football field and I just couldn't make it. The other players jogged passed me and waved. I felt like a slacker even though I was trying as hard as I could to keep up.

Stamina was always a problem even though I took really good care of myself. I wasn't overweight; I didn't smoke or do drugs; and I ate healthy. Although I was frustrated, I blew it off and just plugged along. I often pondered why my stamina was so low. As an active teenager, I should have had plenty of energy but I tended to tire easily. Fortunately, tennis is more of a "short burst energy" kind of sport, so I still excelled. I played through high school and even after having a family.

As I moved in to my twenties and thirties, I began having all kinds of other health issues. I was diagnosed with various ailments, including, fatigue, hypertension, hypoglycemia, recurrent UTI's, unexplained hearing loss, depression, anxiety, etc. I took medications off and on for these ailments but tried to stay off maintenance ones. The only medication that I ended up on long term was for high blood pressure and I didn't start that until I was about 35. At that time, I had four children and two of them were teenagers. I believe that I allowed the normal stress of parenthood to become distress and that took a toll on my health.

Even though I had legitimate health issues I continued to avoid taking additional maintenance medications. The main reason was based on my mother's experiences. She had taken a lot of prescriptions in her lifetime and I really did not want to follow in her footsteps. She experienced many unpleasant side effects and actually lost all of her teeth when she was about forty years old. They simply rotted out within a six month time period. Her doctor told her that it was likely the combination of the fifteen prescriptions that caused it. I would call that a nasty chemical cocktail.

Now, I don't fault my mother for taking all of those medications as she had many health issues. She was trying to get better and followed her doctor's advice. In her day doctors handed out lots of prescriptions with few alternatives. Nowadays, I believe that we are finding alternative solutions that don't have the side effects and I hope this continues. I believe people are waking up to the ills of ingesting too many of these synthetic chemicals, whether in prescriptions or through processed foods and artificial sweeteners. Side effects from medications as well as lawsuits seem to be on the rise. Ultimately, though, the decision is up to the individual.

So, back to my story . . . as I reflected back upon my mother's life, I realized that her ill health paralleled mine in a number of ways. I didn't give it too much thought until later in my illness. The bulk of this information, though, didn't surface until I was writing this book.

She and I both went from being fairly active to living a very sedentary life in a span of just a few short years. While in her thirties my mom had to stop league bowling. According to my father, she just could not grip the ball any longer. For me, hand problems came a little later in life. I was in my forties when I noticed dexterity and strength issues. I also noticed a decline in my agility and stamina even though I was physically fit and playing indoor soccer. Some doctors told me that it was a normal part of aging but I didn't buy it. Our body is designed to function athletically our entire life, as long as we take good care of it.

I also remember that my mother's feet were very sensitive. This is one sign of neuropathy, which is something that I also experienced in my feet. My mother and I both also suffered from balance issues, fatigue, low thyroid, fluid imbalance, sugar disorders, depression and other health issues. Her health continued to deteriorate until she passed away at forty-five from cardiac and respiratory failure.

I never quite understood the circumstances around her death, but my angels helped me with clarification. They showed me what really happened to her and I now have much more compassion for what she went through. For as long as I can remember, my sister and I were led to believe that most of her problems were emotional in nature. We were told that she was mentally ill and I believed that to be her primary problem. I now believe that her primary problem was the same rare disorder that I had and the depression was just secondary.

As I continued to reflect about my early years, I was encouraged to share a couple of stories to show how the divine world interacts with us. I understand more about these events but have probably only scratched the surface of the significance. These interactions are very complex. I feel sure that many of you have had similar experiences but might not have recognized them as being supernatural in origin.

The first story involves a medical crisis that I don't even remember the details of. I just know that I was sick again. I was shuffling along trying to get to the car so I could be transported to the emergency room. I was wearing a pink gown that I had inherited from my mother after she passed away. For some strange reason, I felt like I was actually her, making one of her frequent trips to the hospital. It was just a transient feeling but it certainly was not comforting.

I later disposed of the gown as it brought up too many unhappy feelings that I could not quite understand. I assumed it was just related to a normal memory of that particular unpleasant hospital visit but my angels have said that there is much more to it. Wearing that gown affected me in a negative emotional way and they wanted me to get rid of it. In my mind, I had saved that old pink nightgown thinking that I would feel close to my mother. Instead, it triggered unpleasant memories of her illness and feelings of guilt that I had over our strained relationship.

My angels have taught me that it is good to dispose of items that bring up negative feelings, even if they are still useful. It is simply in our best interest to surround ourselves with things that make us feel happy. Later on, I felt some degree of comfort about my mother's visit after I learned that my husband had also felt her presence. He actually thought he had seen her earlier in the evening. When I learned about this, I felt that she was actually there looking out over me in my time of need. It continues to amaze me that God allows our departed loved ones to provide assistance to those of us still living. With the help of our angels, our loved ones can communicate and even manifest their appearance if it is important enough.

My second story that includes divine interaction is about . . . well, you guessed it . . . another health emergency. I was in post-op after having minor surgery and experiencing quite a bit of pain. My gut feeling was not to take anything so I initially declined medication. I have now learned that the gut feeling is how the divine world communicates with us. It's also called an instinct or a sixth sense. The information is provided to us so that we can make decisions based on it. That world knows what is going to happen and is trying to guide us for our benefit.

Well, I ignored that gut feeling and eventually decided that I should just take something for the pain. I wasn't sure how it would affect me so I asked for a reduced dose. I figured that it would be fine as I was hooked up to all kinds of post-op machinery that monitored my heart and breathing. If something went wrong, surely those monitors would pick it up. And that they did.

I had been given one milligram of morphine and promptly lost consciousness. From what I have been told, one milligram is considered a test dose. For me though, it was too much for my body to handle. Immediately, my heart and respiration rate became very irregular until both completely stopped.

The next thing I remember is vaguely hearing an anxious man saying "Stay with us, now" over and over. He kept talking to me and gently shaking my arm. I also heard several other faint voices in the room and remember wondering what the fuss was all about. I felt so wonderful and wanted everyone to be quiet and just let me sleep! My body was totally relaxed and I felt this amazing sense of peace.

As I opened my eyes, I heard this man talking to me about chest compressions and how my chest might be sore. I remember looking at him and nonchalantly thinking "Oh, okay". I tried to go back to sleep but he continued talking to me and again telling me sharply to "Stay with us, now!" I couldn't figure out what he meant. I heard the room buzzing with activity and then I overheard a conversation. Two nurses were discussing about how I had stopped breathing but my mind still did not process what they were saying.

Shortly thereafter I experienced what I'd now consider a "hot flash like no other". It was if I was going to self combust from the heat. I started yanking my blankets off and noticed that they were very wet. I began to get irritated as I don't like to be wet and I certainly don't like to be hot. I asked what happened to my bedding and someone bluntly replied "You released your bladder".

Now, most folks may not understand this but it took me several more moments to put all those pieces together. Perhaps it was the medication or my temporary state of euphoria, but my brain was not processing well. I pondered over that particular phrase, trying to remember where I had heard it before and what it meant. Then, I suddenly remembered. ONLY DEAD PEOPLE RELEASE THEIR BLADDER. Now, I'm a stickler for detail and I know that is not a completely medically accurate statement but those were my thoughts verbatim at the time.

Instead of going home after my surgery, I ended up spending the night in the special care unit of the hospital. I was hooked up to all kinds of fancy monitors and there was a nice little syringe of an opiate antagonist medication on my bedside table. I guess this was just in case there were residual effects from the morphine. If that wasn't frightening enough, no one was allowed to stay with me overnight and there was no television to distract me. Needless to say, I didn't sleep much that night.

It wasn't until many years later that I learned that my fear during that experience was totally unnecessary (more on this in the chapter about my healing). There will be times when we, as humans, don't have control of our life circumstances. It is important that we turn our fears over to God and let him handle it. He will take care of us.

So, I believe that the divine was at work that December when I coded. I was in the right place to have that experience. I don't fully understand everything that happened but I also believe that the timing was significant. It was a few days before Christmas, our celebration of the birth of Jesus. What a wonderful time to reflect on my spirituality! That particular year I learned to focus less on the gift giving and more about what the holidays truly represent.

I also began to ponder over life and death more. I had always been afraid to die, believing that we simply cease to exist. I thought that we just entered a big void and that was it. After my coding incident, though, I mysteriously lost most of that fear. Even though I do not recall details of a "near death experience", I know that I surely must have had one! Somehow, I had a new comprehension of our soul's transition. We live; we die . . . we live again!

My release from the hospital also coincided with my brother-in-law's birthday, December 19th; his soul's entry into this lifetime. I decided this would be a great time to celebrate my new birthday as well. I did so for several years with my own quiet reflection about what had happened on that day.

For me, the whole experience enlightened me and bolstered my spirituality. Let's face it, at some point in our life, we are all going to lose someone from this physical world. Although it is very difficult for those of us left behind, it is important to know that the departed are going back to be with God and are really not that far away. There is just a very thin veil between heaven and earth.

As you have read, my early years were filled with many odd medical issues. For me, it was a way of life and I simply adjusted to the demands of my body. I just kept on living what I considered to be a normal life. There would become a point though, that I realized the seriousness of my situation.

Chapter Two

The Reality of Illness

In February of 2003, my husband and I celebrated our 25th wedding anniversary. This one was the silver and I was very excited about it. We had married at a young age and many thought we wouldn't make it. Well, we certainly proved them all wrong! We now have been married 36 years!

The best man from our wedding decided to throw us an anniversary party that year. Several other friends pitched in and supplied us with everything that we needed. We had an amazing DJ who provided all of the entertainment and other friends that brought all of the food. Most of our family and friends attended and even our mayor dropped in! I remember feeling good and only having a minimal amount of problems with dexterity. Although we had a nice turnout, one particular person was clearly absent. My mother-in-law, Barbara, had passed away just two months prior to the party.

Barbara was the matriarch of her family and the glue that held everyone together. She was the kind of person that everyone liked and had a heart as big as the state of Texas. She was kind and loving; generous and non-judgmental. After I married her eldest son, we quickly developed the mother-daughter relationship that I desperately needed. She was not only my mother-in-law, but one of my best friends and confidantes.

Barbara's death occurred on what was a significant date for her family and for me. It was on her youngest son's birthday and marked the anniversary of my re-birthday from my coding incident that I shared in Chapter One.

During the evening of December 19th, 2002, friends and family gathered at her home to say their final goodbyes. I know that she was much happier to be at home surrounded by all things familiar. It had been a somewhat lengthy illness and we were all relieved to know that her suffering here on earth was about to end. We sang to her; played her favorite music; and made sure she was comfortable. Although she was heavily medicated, I know she could hear everything around her and appreciated everyone's efforts.

Her exit from this world had an unexpected spiritual affect on me. Although I didn't know it at the time, this experience also served as a prelude to what was in my future. As Barbara was drawing in her last breaths, I began to have these extraordinary visions of her transition from this world!

In my vision, I could see a young Barbara, tall and thin. She looked to be about sixteen years of age and was wearing a grayish colored skirt with a white blouse. She was walking in a misty white tunnel towards a man and a woman who looked very happy to see her. The man and woman were both dressed up and wearing dark colored suits that were from the 1940's era. I immediately recognized them from black and white photographs that I had seen. I could barely believe that I was actually witnessing Barbara's parents welcoming her to heaven!

At about the same time, I had another vision. This time I saw a breathtaking rainbow with several bands of bright and brilliant colors. Now, I've seen plenty of rainbows in my day, but this one was very different. Not only could I see it, but I could actually feel it! This beautiful rainbow emanated the purest form of love that you can possibly imagine. I was filled with this amazing and incredible sense of peace and joy!

I don't know if anyone heard me but I started to whisper about what I was seeing. I so wanted them to feel the same level of comfort that I was feeling. This wonderful person that we all loved dearly was beginning her transition to join her parents and enter a real place! This is a place where there are no constraints of the human body! A place where pain and suffering don't exist! A place that is filled with the purest kind of love that only God can provide! Somehow, I actually got a glimpse into that divine world where we transition from earth into heaven! I was overjoyed that I was allowed to witness something so special!

After her death, I periodically felt like Barbara was trying to connect with me. I frequently dreamed of her even though I was trying not to think about her. Other family members also reported dreaming of her and feeling her presence. One of the younger grandchildren even told her father that her "Nanna" had rocked her to sleep one evening. I was simply amazed that she could still stay so connected!

I am elaborating about Barbara because communication from her was the very catalyst that triggered my clairaudient gift. I'll explain more about how this happened in a later chapter. Although we can communicate with anyone in heaven, I believe that God allows certain spirits to help us in our journey here on earth. I believe that Barbara is one of those spirits. I have no doubt that she is still watching over her family and helping all of us from the other side.

Even though I had an amazing spiritual experience when Barbara died, I began to grieve heavily in the subsequent months. I tried not to but I focused too much on my own personal loss. During this time, my health issues became much more pronounced. The intermittent fatigue worsened and I noticed an increase in dexterity and coordination problems. I allowed the distress to take a toll on my body.

Although I exercised and monitored my food intake, I also rapidly began to gain weight and my face got puffy. It was at this time that I was prescribed thyroid medication. This would be an additional maintenance prescription that I was not real happy about taking. But, I thought it would be the cure that I was looking for. While the thyroid treatment helped me, it didn't completely solve my problems. My symptoms persisted so I began searching for other opinions.

In 2003, I found a wonderful internal medicine doctor that was located close to where I worked. He was just the kind of doctor that I was looking for. His persistence and caring attitude made a huge difference in my outlook. He never gave up looking for answers to what was causing my illness and this was important to me. About the time that I was losing hope, he offered me just the right amount of encouragement. He probably never realized how important his support was to me.

Over the next three years, my symptoms wafted and waned and I had more tests run than you can possibly imagine. Many of them were normal or inconclusive which was quite frustrating. I tried various treatments and did manage to get some temporary relief, though. I sometimes felt like I was on a roller coaster. About the time that I thought I was getting better, I would have a setback. During those times I did get frustrated but I just waited for the next good period to come along. I think it was those intermittent breaks from really severe symptoms that helped me to stay positive.

Even though I was experiencing unusual fatigue and muscle issues, I continued working a full-time job for several more years. Staying busy helped me to keep a sense of normalcy and also kept my mind active. Fortunately for me, my co-workers put up with my occasional pity parties and always offered kind words of encouragement.

Now that I am well I realize how hard it is to be around someone who is suffering from a chronic illness. Sometimes, you just don't know what words will help. It is important, though to always offer positive words.

For those that are ill, it is difficult but very important to always stay in a positive frame of mind. Our mind and body are designed to work together in an amazing synergistic fashion. Our thoughts alone create numerous chemicals that affect our physical body. They contribute to wellness or illness and the choice is ours as to what direction we want to go.

Physical activity was also an important part of my routine. I stayed as active as my body would allow. I had taken up indoor soccer a few years before I really got sick and loved every minute of it. I met some amazing people, including one person that I'll briefly introduce you to here. I'm mentioning Ann in particular because we ended up being kindred souls. Among other things, she actually had a dream about my recovery shortly before it happened! Ann's story is so fascinating that I am planning on including it in another book project tentatively called "Divine Guidance".

In addition to working and playing soccer, I also decided to pursue my education. My step-mother, Marjorie, was my real inspiration here. She returned to school later in life and became quite successful after obtaining her degrees. Since I never saw myself as permanently ill, I thought I would just follow in her footsteps. I was still absolutely convinced that at some point I was going to get well.

I knew that my health issues would make it difficult to maintain a full time job and physically attend classes afterwards but I found a way to work around it. Online courses were available and they were very flexible. Except for a few classes, most of my education was obtained through distance learning. Because of that flexibility, I could work the assignments into my schedule and health needs. Despite the ongoing fatigue, I received my Associates in 2005 and decided to pursue a Bachelor's Degree.

In 2006, I experienced a major turning point in my health. Unfortunately, it was not for the better. It was at that point that my father became quite ill and needed me. During the short time that he was ill, I again forgot to balance relaxation with responsibility. I guess I didn't learn my lesson when my mother-in-law died in 2002. Although it's difficult to balance all of our responsibilities when a loved one needs us, it is very important to do our best. We should make time to do things that we enjoy while caretaking and not feel guilty about it. That is what we need to keep ourselves uplifted and happy.

My father passed away on July 27th of that year to join my mother in heaven. He had lived a long life and I knew that he was ready to go and had been for several months. Although I handled the grief in a healthy manner, my good days became fewer and fewer. This was when I realized that I was no longer on a roller coaster but a very large slide. For the next five years, there were no more up periods, only down ones. Despite this, I kept my chin up and managed to hang on!

Somewhere in this time frame I began another maintenance prescription for sleep issues. I was still trying to work full-time and believed that I needed the medication. When you don't get enough sleep, it is hard to function. I had tried several meditation tapes, but I wasn't getting much relief.

Although this medication should have been taken on a temporary basis, I ended up staying on it for several more years. I tried several times to get off of it as I knew that it was addictive and not good for me, but with no success. What I was unable to accomplish, though, God took care of for me. I'll share more about how this happened in the chapter that deals with my healing. I think that you will find it to be quite fascinating!

About a year after my dad passed away, my weakness and fatigue became so overwhelming that I had to quit playing soccer. This was a major blow for me, albeit a temporary one. I felt like it was admitting some sort of defeat, but it was really quite necessary. I needed to conserve all of my energy so that I could keep working a full time job.

I really had not been participating fully in my games, anyway. It was just too strenuous but I was doing my best to get some exercise. Even though I was not much of an asset, my teammates never let me feel like that. They were very good at picking up my slack and offering me encouragement to keep trying. They were truly good friends to me and I really enjoyed the camaraderie that we all shared.

I also kept going to my games in order to maintain some normalcy. Life for me, though, was becoming anything but normal. There were days that I literally had trouble holding my head up and I was becoming frightened. Simple tasks also began to be difficult. I had to use both of my hands to hold on to a coffee cup and I struggled to wash dishes.

I eventually had to make other adjustments in my life like giving up wearing high heels to work. You might be surprised to know how much muscle strength it takes to walk in those shoes. But, I just replaced my heels with more practical flat shoes and that made my life a whole lot easier. Plus, it was a lot safer for me since I was having balance issues.

My days at work seemed to be getting longer and longer and I began to struggle. Body aches, chills and other intermittent symptoms accompanied the overwhelming fatigue. For the most part, I felt like I had a perpetual case of the flu. Although I went to bed early, I also never felt like I got enough sleep. I really needed about twelve hours of sleep at night to feel fairly rested and that was difficult to do unless it was on the weekend. My lunch hour ultimately became an essential nap hour. Most of the time, this power nap allowed me to finish up the work day.

Towards the end of 2007, though, I just couldn't push any longer. The fatigue was taking its toll and I knew that I needed to rest. I left work for what I believed would be just a few weeks off. Being an eternal optimist, I thought that I would be able to return. Although the extra rest from being home helped somewhat, all of my symptoms continued. No matter what I did, I simply couldn't pull out of the decline. I felt like I was in a tailspin trying to figure out a way to pull out. I continued to do my own research on treatments, though, which helped me feel like I was doing my part to get better.

A few months before I left work, I began seeing a new neurologist that had been highly recommended by another doctor. He was not just any neurologist but a neuromuscular specialist. At the time, I didn't even know that there was a subspecialty within neurology! I got excited as this seemed to be a good fit for me. This doctor had a wonderful reputation as being a doctor who "looks for zebras when he hears hoof beats". Well, by now, I figured that I was a zebra.

I found this new doctor to be quite a fascinating fellow. He talked to me on a level that I could understand which by now was quite technical. During my first visit, he seemed to understand and validated all of my symptoms. He told me that he was pretty sure that he knew what I had and sounded quite confident. At first, I was a little confused. After all of these years, I was going to get a diagnosis? Just like that? For the first time, I really felt like I was going to get treatment and get better. He wanted to run one more specialized test to confirm his suspicions.

When the results of that test came back, he made the diagnosis that explained all of my mysterious symptoms. Finally! After all of the testing and years of frustration, this disorder of mine now had a name and I had hope! In 2007, I was officially diagnosed with a disorder known as a metabolic myopathy.

A metabolic myopathy is a rare muscle disorder that involves some kind of block or dysfunction in the metabolic pathway that creates fuel for skeletal muscles. Inefficient fuel creates symptoms such as muscle fatigue, and weakness. A good analogy is like driving a car with bad gas in it. It will still run, but it runs poorly.

There is also a build-up of toxins that are naturally produced during muscle movement that have nowhere to go. Because of the metabolic block, those toxins cannot be completely processed out of the body. For me, those toxins created intermittent flu-like symptoms such as fatigue, body aches, chills, muscle pain, nausea, weakness, etc. The toxins also take their toll on muscle tissue and it eventually atrophies and becomes weak.

The end result for me was a double whammy. I didn't produce enough fuel for my muscles so they didn't work right. And when I did use them, the movement caused a cascade of chemical reactions that poisoned my body. Well, we need our muscles in everything that we do so not using them was out of the question. I just had to limit what I did so I wouldn't exacerbate the symptoms.

Many of these kinds of illnesses are transparent until late in the disease process. Most people don't even know that you are sick. I realized that there are pros and cons to this invisibility. On one hand, I was glad that I didn't look too bad. On the other hand, I believe that some people, including a few doctors, thought I was making up my symptoms.

Most metabolic myopathies have genetic origins and some can be inherited through the mother's side of the family. They are often misdiagnosed as other more common neurological ailments. Although some are considered treatable disorders, treatment is very limited and not always successful. There is no cure and they are considered to be chronic and progressive.

I originally didn't give much thought to the possibility of having an inherited disorder. I was just glad to be getting treatment. Eventually, I started to do a little more digging into my family tree, though. I was an amateur genealogist so much of the information was already at my fingertips. I also connected with a few family members and started putting the pieces together. I certainly didn't like what I was finding.

One of my cousins on my mother's side had been very ill with numerous disorders throughout her life. She and I were about the same age, which was way too young to be so sick. When we spoke on the phone she also told me that there were many others in the family that were sick. I also knew from my genealogy research that many of my mother's relatives had died very young.

Those ancestors included my mother, grandmother, great-grandmother and great great-grandmother. Initially, I remember thinking about what this meant for me. Only one of those four women made it into their early fifties. Was I a ticking time bomb? The facts stared me in the face, but I decided not to live in fear. I just didn't feel like an early exit was going to be in my future even if the odds were against it.

Eventually, I realized that this could affect my children's health. Out of my four children, my daughter, Kim was always rather sickly. When she was in her mid twenties, I noticed that she was having fatigue and muscle issues. Not too long after that she was diagnosed with having a thyroid condition and I became concerned. Her symptoms were beginning to parallel mine and my mother's. I couldn't keep ignoring what was going on and I contemplated the ramifications.

I now realized that all of my children and grandchildren could develop symptoms similar to mine and I became increasingly alarmed. This certainly was not the legacy that I wanted to leave behind. I again chose not to focus too long on those negative thoughts. The only purpose they served was to fuel my fear and I certainly didn't want or need that. Instead, I ramped up my focus and energies in finding treatment for all of us.

Now, my angels have asked me to include this information so I am going to insert it right here as it has to do with a hereditary link to my illness. As I mentioned earlier, some metabolic myopathies can be inherited through the mother's side of the family. As far as I understand, your mitochondrial DNA or mtDNA is passed down through that line.

One way to look for abnormalities is to do a test called a Mitochondrial DNA Whole Genome Sequencing. I had several genetic tests run, including this one. Although there were no deletions reported, there were a couple of variants that were noted in my results. By themselves, though, I believe that these findings are considered inconclusive. At present, the database is very limited. Perhaps, in the future, my results will yield more information.

I know this is fairly technical for some (and not technical enough for others) but I was urged to include this information. Basically, my results of this test are now stored in a database and I have lots of relatives. I'm not sure if I'm challenging someone to do a study on my family's illness in order to find treatment or whether I'm challenging someone to prove my miracle through science. I guess we will find out when the right reader comes along.

Anyway, I would not be at all surprised if my mtDNA has changed. As a side note, I think I have some muscle tissue stored at two different locations as well. And, I'm tipping my hand here, but some of my relatives have had some interesting improvements in their health as well. I'll cover their stories in a later chapter!

So now that all of the technical stuff is over, let me explain what it is like to live with a metabolic myopathy. I really didn't want to go over all of this, but my angels explained that everyone needs to know this. Maybe it is about finding compassion for others that live with invisible illnesses. Maybe it is to encourage those who are ill to keep on going. Anyway, I can feel my Cherokee roots coming out as this quote came to mind: "Walk a mile in my moccasins and you will know my journey."

Living with a metabolic myopathy can be challenging. For me, ordinary tasks could create severe symptoms and it was difficult to figure out what my limit in activity should be. For example, I could manage to climb a flight of stairs but it subsequently cost me. The activity exacerbated the fatigue, weakness, nausea, body aches, etc. It sometimes took several days to recuperate from climbing just one flight of stairs. It also could take several weeks to recover from other physical activities. Yes, I said weeks. The problem was that it was difficult to determine what kinds of activities would create symptoms.

My sleep requirement eventually increased to over twelve hours each night plus a nap or two. Many times I struggled to just stay awake. I don't know if it was entirely the disorder or a side effect of one of the medications, but it was very real and very frustrating. It was sometimes a difficult challenge, but I managed to schedule activities around my sleep needs.

Eventually, doctors added the diagnosis of fibromyalgia because I began experiencing severe muscle and joint pain. It may be hard for most of you to understand, but even sitting in a hard chair or placing my own hands in my lap created discomfort. I made a few adjustments, though, and kept a lot of pillows around me. I decided not to let the pain get in my way as I had several grandchildren that needed to be loved.

When the pain did get too unbearable, though, I reluctantly agreed to take another medication. This would make my eighth maintenance prescription and may have very well been the worst one for my body. I was also taking numerous vitamins and supplements, all under the advice of my physicians. Many of these had to be taken in multiple doses so I felt like all I did was swallow pills. My pill container eventually became about the size of a sheet of notebook paper.

I don't know for sure what caused the fibromyalgia but it could have been from the progression of the illness. There is also the real possibility that it was caused by a side effect of all the other medications. Any kind of chemical, whether it is prescriptions or even artificial sweeteners, can hamper the body's ability to operate efficiently and heal itself, thus leading to illness. It is also important to remember that toxins are not always immediately lethal. Many can accumulate, thus posing toxicity at a later time.

Although life was very challenging, I decided not to let the illness interfere too much. Whoever said "necessity is the mother of invention" had it right. My neuromuscular doctor inspired me to figure out ways to do all sorts of things. Who knew that adding six inch legs to a couch could make such a difference!

Although my doctors knew this was a serious illness, they stayed very positive and upbeat. I don't remember asking about my prognosis and they spared me the information. Common sense told me that it wasn't good. We need our muscles in everything that we do. That includes basic stuff like breathing. I was aware that my illness was considered to be chronic progressive and that you don't recover from it. Late in the illness, I began having visual disturbances and I had trouble swallowing. It was then that I equated my illness to a slow Lou Gehrig's. I really wasn't afraid, though, but stayed focused on getting well. I just figured out a way to manage the symptoms as they progressed.

I also decided not to give up on my dreams. At the time I left work on disability in 2007, I was only a few classes short of my Bachelor's Degree. Since the online classes are not physically demanding, I decided that I would just finish it! The coursework was flexible so I just completed the assignments on my good days. I remember thinking that the degree would help me if I went back to work. I guess I was still holding on to those positive thoughts!

In 2008, I graduated Summa Cum Laude from Texas Woman's University. Just so you don't have to look that up, it means that I graduated at the top of my class with highest honors. Although I experienced some trepidation about the length of the diploma line, I managed to complete the long walk! Finally! After thirty years, I got the diploma that I had been dreaming of! It is never too late to pursue an education, even if it is just to broaden your horizons!

Even though I was limited, my husband and I continued to take our annual vacations. I initially hesitated as I feared that the travel could jeopardize my benefits. I decided to not worry about this. The travel gave me something to look forward to and I enjoyed the change in scenery. During those trips, I simply rested as much as possible. I did suffer a few health repercussions, but the positives always outweighed the negatives.

Since my healing, I have learned a few things about faith and financial benefits. Many honest people have a real fear that they will lose their disability benefits if they do certain things, like travel. The fear is that the government or corporations are just looking for ways to deny them what is justly theirs.

There is some truth to that statement, but keep this in mind. The honest will be rewarded and I'm not talking about the after-life. God will provide for them financially here on earth. It is important to be patient and trust Him. I have learned to always trust God in these matters and to let go of all worries. Society is not always fair but He makes sure that the repercussions are fair. Just remember that He knows everything. Again, the honest will be rewarded.

As far as traveling, it's important for those who are ill to continue to lead as normal a life as possible. This means continuing to travel and keep social engagements as health allows. It lifts the soul and improves mood. This, in turn, improves overall health. So, basically, I

The Reality of Illness

made the right decision and continued to go on vacations. It did lift my mood and I also had some very interesting experiences during those trips.

In 2007, my husband and I were in Monroe County, Tennessee and actually got to see a crop circle! It was quite interesting on how we found it. We had stopped at a convenience store and I noticed a picture of a crop circle on a local newssheet. I asked the sales clerk if he knew where it was located and I was told that it was right there in that very county! That was all it took to ignite the investigator in me!

I got directions to the local police department to see if they could give me its exact location. As I entered the police department I felt like I had stepped back in time. It was just a small department where everyone seemed relaxed and on a first name basis with all of the locals. I bravely made my inquiry, half expecting them to make fun of me. Instead, they made a phone call and told me exactly where to find it! As it turned out, we were only minutes away!

We followed their directions and realized that it was going to be very difficult to see a crop circle from ground level. All we could really see were wheat fields and a few houses. We were just about to give up when we saw a young woman getting groceries out of her car. We stopped and asked her if she knew anything about it. I was flabbergasted when she said it was directly across the street and she would be happy to show it to us! How about that for perfect timing!

We found out later that a crop circle investigation group filed a report claiming that this circle was genuine and not man-made! Among other things, there were abnormal radiation amounts detected and the wheat structure was unusual. It also appeared to be in a woven design. I found it quite fascinating when I learned that this one was in the shape of a double Celtic cross! The following year another crop circle was reported nearby within the same county and the same group investigated it. This time, they came up with completely different results and concluded that one to be man-made.

I have to say that the paranormal has always fascinated me so coming across that crop circle was an extraordinary find. I don't believe that it was simply by chance but felt like I was guided right into it. There are experiences put before us in our lives for our learning and enjoyment. These are gifts from God. Pay attention so you don't miss them!

During that same trip, something else interesting happened. While at a scenic overlook, I met a man that looked just like my father. I know that someone out

The Reality of Illness

there is thinking that we all have a twin here on earth and this is no big deal.

But, I don't believe in coincidences. I was overwhelmed with the feeling that there was much more to this meeting. This fellow and I have since stayed in contact, trying to get to the bottom of the mystery. I believe that he is just as intrigued as I am! All of the circumstances and logistics lead me to one conclusion. Time will tell, but it is very possible that he is my brother from another mother! Don't forget that our angels will guide us into these encounters if they are important.

In 2009, I decided to take another trip. A neighbor had inspired me to go to the renowned Mayo Clinic in Minnesota. He was getting ready to go there to search for treatment for his own unusual illness. I was still declining and looking for a better treatment so I made my plan to go.

I don't think that it was by chance that my neighbor shared that information with me. We bumped into each other one day while I was outside trying to take a walk. At that point, it was unusual for me to do so. He happened to be jogging past me and we stopped to chat.

As it turned out, he was eventually diagnosed with the Lou Gehrig's that I had feared. I don't know what it all means but I continue to pray for his recovery. He is also a prayer warrior and very determined. I look forward to hearing about his progress as he has currently surpassed all medical expectations.

After a week of testing at the Mayo Clinic, doctors there didn't have any more answers for me. I returned home somewhat disheartened but by no means ready to completely accept my illness. That was when I realized that I was officially suffering from slight depression and decided to do something about it. I vetoed suggestions that I add an anti-depressant to the mix of medications that I was already on and decided to add talk therapy instead. Medications can only make a dent in depression treatment and can have permanent repercussions. There are all kinds of other treatments available that don't have the dangerous side effects of prescriptions.

I had decided even before going to the Mayo Clinic that my visit there would be my last effort at finding help through traditional medicine. The logical part of me wanted to make sure that I had done everything possible to find answers within that community. I think this gave me some peace of mind. In a weird way, I found myself much more relaxed when I got home. It was during this period of relaxation that I decided to regroup and form a new plan.

Chapter Three

A Friend in Need

Friends are those people in our lives that we choose to build enjoyable relationships with. Some are with us for a few seasons and some are in our lives for a lifetime. Or, if you believe like me, some can be with you in several lifetimes. Whichever way it is, we should cherish all of those relationships.

Lifetime friends are very dear and special ones, even if you don't see each other often. I met one of my lifetime friends when I was about eleven years old and we are still best friends today. The first encounter with her that I remember was on the bus while on our way home from school. She was the new girl in town and there was something very special about her.

LeAnn was the type of person that didn't know a stranger. She was friendly and outgoing and always had a smile on her face. We started chatting on the bus that day and haven't stopped since. We quickly became good friends and shared some really fun times together. I sometimes wonder if our instant bond wasn't something more ethereal; perhaps we are soul sisters that have traveled together through other lifetimes.

Anyway, after returning from the Mayo Clinic in 2009, I decided to have a birthday party. I was turning 50 that year and I considered that a milestone. The planning process lifted my mood considerably. I expected that I would get a better attendance to this shindig than the pity parties that I had been having before. Sure enough, I had a good turnout and LeAnn even made a special trip in from Dallas.

LeAnn and I had shared a few other interesting birthdays together through our years of friendship. One involved an open sunroof and some woo-woo's, but we won't talk about that one. There were other celebrations that were much more memorable. One of them involved the Eiffel Tower and a bottle of champagne.

In February of 2010, LeAnn took several of her closest friends to Europe to celebrate her 50th birthday. My hubby and I were among those friends. He and I had been discussing taking a trip to Europe for years. We had wanted to visit Italy, where his mother's family was from. I kept waiting for finances to get better and my health to improve but neither seemed to be happening. And then it simply materialized! LeAnn's generosity took care of the finances part as she simply added Italy to her birthday trip. It was just the nudge that I needed so off we went!

We began the trip in Paris to fulfill LeAnn's dream of a birthday toast under the Eiffel Tower. Even though it was rather chilly, it was an awesome experience! We spent a few more days in Paris and on a hot path to see as many sites as possible. Among those were the Notre Dame Cathedral and the Basilica Sacre-Couer. The walking was quite hard on me but I just rested when I could. Perhaps it was the change in climate or the adrenaline, but I found a way to keep on going.

Although I loved Paris, I had really wanted to travel to Lourdes for holy water. Lourdes, which is located in the south of France, is well known as a place to find miracles and I was looking for one. I didn't think that I would ever be able to get back to Europe and figured this was my one shot. It ended up being too far as there wasn't enough time for me to make the journey. I also wasn't well enough to trek out on my own. I was disappointed about not being able to go but decided not to dwell on it.

I didn't realize at that time that there are many other holy places located all around the world. It's important that they are accessible to everyone. I have also learned that it is not necessarily a prerequisite to visit them to receive a healing. If it is important enough for us to visit one for inspiration, though, God and our angels will make sure that we get what we need. More on this later!

After our short stay in Paris, we moved on to the Tuscany area for the second leg of the trip. One of my biggest fears on this adventure was that I would slow everyone down. I had been feeling quite ill since the second day in Paris and really needed some rest. Interestingly enough, LeAnn had not made any plans for one entire day while in Italy. We were staying at a villa where we all kicked back and relaxed for a day. It was the perfect opportunity for me to recharge my batteries!

During our day of rest, the two of us also got to enjoy some quality time together. As I was perusing through the living room of the villa, I noticed a stack of board games. One in particular caught my eye. It was a Scrabble game! You may be wondering why I got so excited, but LeAnn and I have a long history of Scrabble games. We rarely get to play as we live in two different cities, so this was a real treat for both of us.

This may not seem like a big deal to most folks, but finding that Scrabble game was rather intriguing to me. Here we were in a different country and there was our favorite board game. Some would say that this was just a coincidence, but I don't believe it! I'm convinced that the divine was at work here again to bring us that little bit of extra enjoyment!

While in the Tuscany area, we visited the walled city of Lucca which was where my husband's ancestors were from. Inside the walls, there were many small old churches. Prominent people or religious figures were sometimes buried within the building itself.

The church that I remember most vividly was San Frediano's. While wandering around we came across a very interesting coffin. It was made of glass and was above the ground on display. Inside of it was the body of St. Zita, a local woman who evidently did not decompose after death. The Catholic definition of this phenomenon is incorruptibility and is believed to be from the divine touch of God. I don't recall exactly how they figured out that she wasn't decomposing but remember the story was quite fascinating. It was a rather strange sight, but even after 700 years, St. Zita was amazingly well preserved and even had fingernails still intact!

Within this same church, something very interesting happened. I actually caught a glimpse of what I believe was an apparition near one of the crypts. Out of the corner of my right eye, I saw what looked like white smoke. It was quite hazy but I could determine that it was in the shape of a spiral and quite long.

As I turned to get a better look, it quickly whirled out a window. I thought I might have seen a reflection since I wear glasses and it does happen. I quickly snapped some pictures anyway, hoping to catch something unusual. Nothing suspicious showed up so I didn't mention anything to anyone.

During dinner that evening, though, my husband and I had a very interesting conversation. He asked me if I had seen anything unusual in that same chapel. Of course, I didn't tell him about my experience and just asked him to tell me what he saw.

Needless to say, I got very excited when he told me that he thought he had seen an apparition and his description matched mine exactly! There is no way that we would have both imagined the same phenomenon so I have no doubt that it was real! Perhaps we even saw St. Zita! Just like other saints, she is definitely associated with miracles! As I mentioned in the previous chapter, there are some pretty amazing experiences placed before us!

A Friend in Need

The final leg of our European trip was reserved for a quick visit to the magnificent city of Rome. We didn't get to see much but we did manage to visit a few places. We quickly toured the museum at the Vatican as well as the Sistine Chapel. We then made our way into St. Peter's Basilica. It wasn't on the planned itinerary but ended up being a spontaneous stop at the request of my husband. I sure am glad he suggested it!

St. Peter's Basilica is supposed to be where Simon Peter, one of the apostles of Jesus, is buried. According to strong historical evidence, he is buried directly under the altar. Well, I guess you could say that they built the altar over where he is supposed to be buried. I didn't know anything about this while I was there, but I did feel very drawn to that altar.

I also felt very close to God while I was there. Actually, I was overwhelmed with emotion as soon as we entered. The jaw dropping splendor of this place created a wonderfully amazing atmosphere. The ceiling of the basilica stood several stories high and included a taller domed area that was directly above the altar. Most of it was painted to perfection with exquisitely rich and vibrant colors.

Everywhere you looked, there was something magnificent to behold. There were many huge marble pillars and statues filled every niche. Some areas had a heavy casing of gilt which added to the feeling of richness. There were also beautiful paintings and other fine works of art strategically positioned throughout the entire building.

The shape of the building itself was somewhat confusing to me as there didn't appear to be any uniformity to it. As I found out later, part of the interior is devoted to altars and tombs for former popes. Each one of these burial areas was a unique masterpiece in itself. Initially, I didn't even realize that these were burial sites. It is really not surprising that I felt such a strong spiritual presence!

For me, visiting St. Peter's Basilica was the highlight of our trip to Rome. I'm not Catholic but I felt that this church was one of God's special places. I have mixed emotions about the opulence but believe that it is necessary, to a degree. The magnificence of some of these churches can be considered akin to being in heaven where beauty is everywhere. I think most of us would like to visit a little piece of heaven every once in awhile.

I also think that sometimes God has to pull out all the stops to get us to a holy place. I believe that the extravagant design is very intentional. The beauty of these places is what draws most of us. We want to see the tall elaborately painted ceilings and admire those fantastic stained windows. And while we are there, we accidentally begin thinking about God.

On the other hand, there are also wonderfully spiritual places that are mostly unadorned. They are tucked away in small communities and for the most part, go unnoticed. I happened to "stumble" in to one of those places about five months later.

In July of 2010, LeAnn asked me to go on another trip with her. The circumstances this time were quite different. She was in New Mexico on business and going through a rough personal crisis. I was really shook up when I heard her voice. She asked me to fly out to Santa Fe as she needed me. Never in the forty years of our friendship, had she asked me for anything. I knew that this was important.

So after the tearful call, I made my plan. I was concerned about traveling with my physical limitations and shared this with my husband. I leaned on him fairly heavy in those days as I didn't like to be anywhere alone. He simply replied, "You can do it". Well, that bolstered my confidence and off to the airport we went. He dropped me off and I realized that I was alone.

Many of you may not understand this, but I was afraid. At any given moment, I could run out of gas and there would be no one to help me. My disorder was so rare that it would take forever to explain what I had if I needed medical help. Even at that, most doctors wouldn't believe me anyway. My own internal medicine doctor told me that it was a diagnosis that was "way above his pay grade".

But, when your best friend sends out an SOS, you don't hesitate. I wasn't about to let her down. So, I mustered up my courage and dragged my suitcase all by myself to the gate. For just a little while, I was independent again.

LeAnn appeared to be in better spirits when I got there so I was relieved. We went to one of her business functions and she seemed to be like her old self again. We really never talked much about what was bothering her but it didn't matter. She needed my physical presence and moral support more than intense conversation.

I never thought that I would like the atmosphere in New Mexico as I pictured it as all dust and dirt. I was pleasantly surprised to find out that this was not entirely true. Santa Fe has a lot of appeal and such an interesting charm to it! While there, I managed to visit several little shops on my own. I was on the hunt for souvenirs and Christmas presents. I paced myself and just rested along the way. The arid climate was a big plus for me, too, as it alleviated a great deal of my pain. It never occurred to me that this was a divinely orchestrated trip.

On our last day in New Mexico, LeAnn and I trekked out to do some sightseeing. After a relaxing lunch, we took off and drove thirty minutes north of Santa Fe. The destination was to see a small Spanish chapel called El Santuario de Chimayo. She chose this one because it was the only one in the area that she had not been to yet.

The first thing I noticed when we got to this place was the abundance of shrines and crosses. They were everywhere! Not only were there formal crosses, but small handmade ones all over the place. They were attached to the fencing and fastened to almost all of the trees. Most of them that I saw were made of small twigs and very rustic looking.

We strolled around the grounds and eventually made our way to the small chapel. I was moved by how charming it was. Surrounding the chapel was this old looking adobe wall that protected a small courtyard. The wall was about four foot high and had several entrances. The main one had these two large rustic wooden doors that really caught my eye.

Those two doors sat somewhat askew as if they had fallen slightly off their hinges. It seemed as if their permanently open position represented an invitation for all to enter. On each side of the doors there was a beautiful climbing rose bush that further enhanced the charm. It was all so very picturesque and had such a cozy feel to it.

As I looked at those awesome doors, I began to take in the rest of the scenery. I first noticed the outline of the top of the chapel and how interesting it looked against the bright blue sky. To top it off there were these really cool mountains in the background that were speckled green with what I guess were shrubs. I felt such a wonderful sense of peace, as if the mountains were somehow protecting us from the rest of the world.

My gaze then shifted back to the chapel itself. The entire building looked to be made of adobe with a little bit of woodwork and a tin roof. It had a very quaint and balanced look to it with two small crosses sitting atop two matching bell towers. There was some kind of unusual wooden ladder on the roof that must have given access to each tower.

The actual doorway to the chapel was somewhat inconspicuous but nonetheless intriguing. We ventured inside and the first thing that I noticed was it was really dark. Of course, it was a bright sunshiny day so my eyes had to adjust. I then began to study the interior of this interesting little place.

I don't remember seeing any windows but there were a lot of brightly colored paintings all over the walls. It was kind of like they replaced the stained glass windows that you would find in a traditional church. It was such a stark contrast to the cathedral we had just seen in Rome a few months earlier.

At the very front of this chapel was a very interesting six foot crucifix that appeared to be made of wood. The crucifix and everything around it were also decorated with really bright and cheerful colors. I later learned a very interesting story about that cross that I'll share a bit later. I'm sure that you will enjoy it as it certainly adds to the intrigue of this place!

LeAnn and I took a seat on one of the front pews to further soak up this unusual atmosphere. We sat in silence and after a few moments of thoughtful reflection, I began to look around again. It was at this point that I noticed a doorway off to the left. Something caught my eye but I can't remember exactly what it was. It may have been the lit candles. Whatever it was, it beckoned me to further investigate.

Curious, I rose from the pew and entered the side room. This room was also very colorful and I noticed that there were crosses and crucifixes everywhere here as well. It was a fairly narrow room with one entire wall papered with letters and photographs. It was if the walls were bulletin boards and one could place anything they wanted to on them.

I kept looking around as I was confused to the meaning of it all. When I saw that the opposite wall was lined with crutches, walkers, canes, and braces, I began to get excited. This was not just an ordinary place. This was a place where miracles happen!

I was then drawn to the back of the room where there was an inconspicuous little doorway. This doorway was rather short so I had to bend over to enter it. And then I saw it. It was just a small unassuming hole in the ground filled with ordinary looking dirt. Inside that hole was also a little yellow plastic shovel. I tried to stay calm as I fumbled in my purse for a container. I quickly dumped out my snack bag and attempted to kneel down to get some dirt.

I hesitated and looked down at that hole. I knew that the possibility of injuring a muscle was very real and it would cost me dearly to squat down. Using those muscles would start a cascade of chemical reactions in my body and I would feel very ill very quickly.

I started to get the dirt but stopped. I realized that it would be very foolish of me to squat down when there was another woman in the room with me that could help. I let go of my pride and asked her for assistance. She filled my little plastic bag with holy dirt and I carefully tucked it in my purse.

Unbeknownst to me, this was the beginning of one incredible journey. A new chapter was unfolding for me; one where anything is possible. I had wanted to visit Lourdes for a miracle and there I was. You see, I had just visited a place that is known as the Lourdes of America. I told you that God makes sure that we get what we need.

Chapter Four

Other Methods of Healing

While doing research for this chapter, I realized that there was a shift in my search to get well after visiting Chimayo, New Mexico. It wasn't a dramatic shift, but I can see how I changed. Before I explain about that shift, I want to go over some of the methods that I had been using to get well before that.

Before Chimayo, I mainly looked for answers to heal myself within the traditional method of healing (although I occasionally considered a few alternative treatments). Most of it was based around taking prescription medications. Well, I took what was prescribed and it wasn't working at getting me better. As a matter of fact, I believe that some of those prescriptions actually did quite a bit of harm to me.

I want to elaborate a little here because I think it's important to make a few points about this. I don't fault the doctors for prescribing those medications. This was

Other Methods of Healing

how they were taught to help heal their patients. And I'm the one that agreed to take them. I think it would have been better, though, if they had suggested natural alternatives instead of the drugs that they prescribed.

It is very important to remember that our medicines can be generated by our own body or found in our foods. For example, laughter creates "happy brain chemicals" that affect our mood. Even smiling changes our brain chemistry for the better! And don't forget about prayer! (Okay, I do believe that my angels inserted that last message).

And, while I'm on this topic, I'd like to make another point. I'm generalizing here, but I believe that most doctors don't hand out prescriptions until they feel it is absolutely necessary. Their first line of recommendation to their patient is usually to eat healthier, lose weight, exercise and stop smoking. I think that we have heard this so many times, that it has become a joke within our society. But many people completely ignore this advice.

In reality, this is the absolute cure for good health! But, if you have a patient that won't follow these instructions, what options do you have? You could refuse to treat them which is what some doctors do. Or, you can keep encouraging them to make changes and give them a prescription to treat whatever illness that they came in with. I believe that the goal for many doctors at this point is to try and help their patient to preserve a decent quality of life.

Well, I have said my spill so I'll get back on topic. Before Chimayo, I also made a few other changes within my life that would still be considered traditional methods at getting well. I analyzed what I was eating again to see if there could be anything affecting my health.

For the most part, I was eating fairly healthy as I knew the ramifications of an unbalanced diet. There were a few times in my younger years that I unsuccessfully tried a fad diet or two. One in particular involved omitting a food group. You may not believe this, but I ended up in the emergency room over that as well. Your body really needs all of the food groups to run efficiently. Leaving out any of them for an extended period of time causes great distress to your system. That distress will lead you right into an illness.

While reviewing my diet, I only found one substance that I believed could be potentially unhealthy for me. It was an artificial sweetener that I had ingested for many years. I made the switch over to a sugar substitute, believing it to be a natural product. Well, like many consumers, I believe that I was misled by marketing. It was not a natural substance and was not much better than the other stuff that I had been ingesting.

Since I have been healed, I really try to stress the importance of giving up all synthetic sweeteners. They are a huge problem for our society and can cause a variety of health issues. I equate this to putting bad gas in your car. In the beginning, it will still run, but less efficiently. Eventually, if you keep using that bad fuel, your car will give out completely. I think you get my drift.

In addition to giving up artificial sweeteners, I was also guided into using honey. There are other healthy sweetening alternatives available but my angels knew that this would become my favorite. There are also a great number of medicinal benefits to honey that my body may have needed. Our angels really know how to lead us to just the right foods to help us get better!

So, after switching sweeteners (that's a mouthful, isn't it?), I decided to order a couple of biochemistry books. I never really enjoyed chemistry but I was determined to learn how I could heal my body through food. Really, the premise is not that unusual. Our bodies are chemical factories and mine wasn't running right. I figured if I could add the right ingredients, I could bypass the block that was creating my problems.

I was going to do my research and then consult with my physician to make sure the dietary changes would be safe for me. As it turned out, though, I never even had to crack those books open!

Another avenue that I pursued to get well involved hypnosis. I knew that sometimes childhood emotional issues could contribute to illness. Well, I thought I had dealt with my issues but thought it was worth a try.

I searched out my longtime friend and therapist to see if she could help. We had met many years ago when I was addressing stress issues. I don't believe that it was a coincidence that she was brought into my life. She has helped me immensely through the years work through normal life issues.

Anyway, my therapist, Sandra, didn't believe that there were any childhood issues that were a problem for me but she agreed to give it a try. Our session didn't reveal anything interesting but it did lead us into another area of healing. We put together a visual imagery healing script and she recorded it for me to listen to on a daily basis.

Now, this is where I believe the subtle shift may have happened. You see, a healing script would be considered a non-traditional method of curing ourselves. From that point on, my focus became less on traditional medicine and more towards a spiritual path to healing.

A healing script consists of a few brief paragraphs that describe a healing going on within the body. It should be customized for each individual using wording and analogies that trigger an emotional response for that person. It can be recorded, memorized or read aloud, but should be done every day. While listening to it, one should imagine the actual events taking place within the body. This is what is called visual imagery and is a useful technique for healing.

During the session you use your "mind's eye" to visualize changes going on within your body. It is also a form of meditation and promotes relaxation and positivity about becoming well. This thought process releases certain chemicals within the brain that can have positive physiological effects on the body. There can also be a spiritual aspect of this technique if you incorporate nature within the healing session.

I ended up tweaking out the script that Sandra made to one that I responded better to. It's important to use these kinds of scripts as a framework and personalize them to your own needs. I had to visualize several different scenarios of healing to see which one made me feel better.

In one scenario, I imagined that I was laying on a big flat rock in a shallow gently flowing river, allowing the water to wash away my illness. The rock felt good as it was nice and warm but I kept thinking that I was going to drown. Since I wasn't completely feeling relaxed or powerful, I came up with another visual.

In this scenario, I just imagined that I was a tree and my arms were the branches. I raised my arms and reached up into the sky with my "branches" and pulled down the strength of the sun to heal my body. I remember how good it felt to stretch and reach out for healing. I allowed my open hands to pass over my body, covering it with the healing energy of the sun. I then closed my fists and centered my strength within my abdomen.

After I had filled my body with the healing energy of the sun, I began to focus on clearing away the illness. During the clearing, I took my hands and magically waved them over my entire body, ending at my feet which were the roots of my tree. I then imagined releasing all of my toxins through my roots and watching an underground river carry away the illness. I remember thinking that Mother Earth was strong enough to handle this illness!

Other Methods of Healing

I repeated this process a minimum of three times or until I felt like I was making some progress. There were days that I wasn't feeling very powerful, though, so I came up with an additional visualization. After reaching upwards and gathering strength from the sun, I imagined pulling up additional strength from the ground. After each movement, I centered it at my abdomen or core with my hands closed into a fist. After I felt strong enough, I would start the process of clearing the illness out of my body. I think this would be a good visual imagery for most people. It's not hard to imagine feeling the warmth of the sun and the strength of the earth beneath your feet.

Although visual imagery promotes the physical relaxation that we need to heal, it is also a spiritual method of healing. Although I don't remember thinking about God directly, I was focused on His sun for healing (Hmmm, an angel guided Freudian slip?). At any rate, my visual imagery with the tree increased my spirituality and that made me feel better.

For those readers who want to try this technique, I recommend that you customize it to what makes you feel the best. Think about a place that you love to be at and come up with your own healing scenario. Make the process fairly brief so that you will be more likely to practice it regularly. If we make it too complicated and long, we are less likely to do it. Also, it would be a good idea to incorporate your own form of prayer or request for assistance. I think this helps us to feel better and more connected to the divine world. It doesn't have to be formal or long, just heartfelt. It is a phenomenal feeling to know that you are connected with a higher power!

Another avenue that I pursued to get well combined spirituality with mainstream healing. I have always believed that psychics were privy to other worldly information so I searched out a few of them. My goal was to see if they could direct me to the right clinic or doctor for treatment. I guess I wasn't entirely thinking about a supernatural healing, just supernatural advice!

The first psychic/intuitive that I discovered became a really good friend of mine. Donna and I originally met in 2003 when I was in the early throes of my illness. I know that our meeting was not a chance encounter so I'll share how it happened here with you. After my mother-in-law passed away in 2002, I kept feeling like she was trying to connect and tell me something. For awhile, I dreamed about her almost every night and I was concerned that I was missing a message. I was also looking for answers about my illness.

I searched the local ads to find a psychic but had no success. One day while I was still working I decided to pick up a sandwich and go out for lunch. The plan was to sit near the beach and just relax. What is interesting is that I had never done this before. I don't even really care for the beach that much.

But, I parked my car near the beach and ate my lunch. I decided to get out and do a little shopping while I was there. There was this really cool building that was over the water and I noticed that it had some new little shops within it. For you history buffs, that building was the Balinese Room in Galveston, Texas that was destroyed in Hurricane Ike in 2008. If you are interested, the Balinese Room has its own legendary stories that are well worth reading about.

Anyway, I wandered around and noticed a window display that caught my eye. Before I entered the shop, I noticed a sign posted on the door. I think my heart skipped a beat as it said "Psychic Readings by Appointment". Well, I didn't believe in coincidences back then and knew that I had been led to this place by some unseen force. This was exactly what I was looking for and here it was in my own backyard!

I met with Donna later that day and we have remained good friends ever since. During my reading, she successfully connected with my mother-in-law and that gave me the comfort that I needed. She also gave me helpful and extremely accurate information about my living family members. I feel sure that the information helped me to make some positive adjustments in my relationships with them. Although she did not come up with the specifics on how I could get well, she did let me know that I was doing everything right.

In retrospect, I realize that all of the information about my health was not supposed to be revealed just yet. Donna had an amazing connection with the divine world and was very accurate about everything that she told me. She actually did tell me what was going on with my body but it was too vague for me to do anything about. She told me that I was " . . . eating right but I wasn't getting everything". She also mentioned " . . . like an amino acid."

Well, I have to say that this was a very close explanation to what I would eventually be diagnosed with. I know that if it had been important enough at the time, she would have come up with the wording for that diagnosis. It must have been more important for me to go on the journey.

Later on in that journey, I again searched Donna out for help. This was about a year after I went to Chimayo and about four months before my healing. I still believed that there might be a repressed childhood memory that was potentially interfering with my healing. I had some blank spots in my memory and I wasn't sure if it was important. At that point, I was not going to leave any stone unturned in my search to get well.

By now, Donna had moved out of state but I didn't let that stop me. Our funds were limited but I had a strong feeling that this was an important trip. We set up a date for my visit and I began making travel arrangements. Because of the extreme fatigue and muscle issues, I knew that I couldn't travel alone. As it turned out, there was only one person in my family that could make this trip with me. It happened to be the same daughter that was showing signs of the muscle disorder that I had. I can only speculate here, but feel that there was some sort of divine guidance going on to get her there as well.

After we arrived, Donna proceeded to do some hypnosis work with me. She felt guided to do past life regression work rather than the traditional hypnosis that I requested. I trusted her intuition so that is how we proceeded. We spent two days of intensive hypnosis work and uncovered four previous lives that might have been impacting this one. During the sessions, I learned how to release negative emotions such as sadness, humiliation and shame and replace them with love, confidence and pride. I learned how important it is to offer forgiveness, no matter what has happened to you.

When I went back and listened to our recorded sessions, I could actually hear Donna's voice change and take on an ethereal tone that was quite comforting. At that time, I thought that it was a little unusual. I now realize that she was channeling angels during my healing sessions! That was in July of 2011 and by October I would fully understand how it worked. Little did I know that this amazing gift would be in my future, too!

I have a few theories about how past life regression works but don't want to get in to that too much right now. I do believe that it has a place in alternative methods of healing, though, and will become more popular as time goes by. All I know is that I felt much better after our sessions.

I also gathered quite a bit of information during those sessions. As of now, I am planning to include it in another book with the working title "This Cat Has Nine Lives – Plus or Minus a Few". I guess I channeled that book title right after the sessions. You see, "Cat" is my nickname and evidently I have had at least nine previous lives! Keep watching for this one as I believe it will be quite an interesting book!

I had also reached out to another psychic reader for answers prior to my visit with Donna. One of my friends from work recommended this one and I was really hoping that he could help me. He was local to my area so we got together a few times. My goal was to either get information on how to get well or learn how to get the information myself.

During our first session, there was a lot of information revealed that didn't entirely make sense at the time. After my healing, I went back and listened to the recording again and was thoroughly impressed by his accuracy. Most of his information for me was prophetic which obviously can't be verified at the time of the reading.

I haven't been able to reconnect with him but would love to let him know how on target he really was. Many psychics/readers/intuitives don't get validation of their "hits" until their clients' later share the information with them. There were several pieces of really interesting information that did manifest within the next two years!

One of his visions involved a "little girl" that was repeatedly changing her clothes, as if she was playing dress-up. I couldn't figure out how that pertained to me. I had been scaling down my wardrobe and simplifying my life. Changing clothes just took too much of my limited energy. That vision now makes perfect sense to me. I love clothes and work hard at finding the right outfits that make me feel good. I look for unusual clothing, shoes, hats and other accessories to find my own unique look. Some of my favorite finds have even been at resale shops or discarded items from friends! And yes, on most days, I will change clothes at least one time to see if it fits my mood for the day!

On that same note, I am being informed (by you know who) that we should discard those clothing items that affect our mood in a negative manner when we wear them. There are plenty of good inexpensive clothes and accessories at resale establishments to replace what has been given away! For those creative folks, though, be sure and take another look to see if you want to retrieve any cool looking trim, lace or other embellishment for a future project!

The second interesting piece of information that was revealed during my reading concerned a lawsuit in my future. He informed me that there were going to be two females involved and they were both attorneys. I was going to have a problem with one of them and she was not to be trusted. The other one appeared to him and said "I've got this one".

He further told me that it was going to be a civil suit against me. He saw it as quite a shock to me but said that everything would be okay. I remember thinking at the time "Why on earth would anyone want to sue me?"

And guess what. True to his prediction, I was sued and there were female attorneys on both sides of the case. I will admit here that he was spot on in that it was one of the biggest shocks that I have ever received.

I have to say that I went through a variety of emotions. Right after the initial shock, I was frightened. This was a serious suit that could cost my husband and I everything that we had left. We were already in a financial strain with only a limited amount of resources. Then, shortly after that I became angry and indignant. I knew that I didn't deserve what was happening to me.

But, my angels calmed me down and reassured me that everything would be okay. They instructed me on what to do and to remember a few things. Even though there are circumstances in our lives that are unfair, God will make sure that all is evened out. I would not suffer financially and what was due me would be forthcoming.

They also reminded me that it was in my best interest to offer forgiveness to anyone and everyone that I felt had wronged me. Well, true to my psychic friend's prediction, the dispute was resolved without major ramifications. And yes, I have forgiven everyone concerning this matter. There are always extenuating circumstances and sometimes certain situations cannot be avoided.

At any rate, it is important not to worry about those things that we cannot control. Ahhh, that brings me to the serenity prayer! Although there are many versions, the meaning is about the same in all of them. Here is the version that my father loved to share:

God grant me the serenity

to accept the things that I cannot change;

the courage to change those that I can;

and the wisdom to know the difference.

Well, I have digressed again so it must have been important. Another interesting piece of information that was mentioned during my reading concerned a brother. I had not told my psychic friend about my belief that I had a brother from another mother. But, he kept envisioning a guy with his thumb up saying "Hey, this

Other Methods of Healing

brother's got your back". I'm still trying to figure out the significance of this information but feel that time will surely tell!!

The last piece of information that was shared that day had me completely dumbfounded. He told me that people would be coming to see me from all over and that I would be healing them with my words. Well, this made absolutely no sense to me. At that point, I was handicapped and barely able to get up the few steps that it took to get to his place of business. Plus, I was fifty years old and not even remotely considering a new career!

But, here again, he was completely accurate in his prediction! I am now doing my own readings and working with people who need healing. I operate out of my own shop that is located on the beautiful island of Galveston, Texas. People visit from all over the world because it is an ideal tourist location. And, many have mysteriously found their way into my little shop!

Although I received a lot of good information that day, I still didn't have the information that I wanted. Here again, it must not have been time for it to be revealed. I was a little frustrated with the lack of answers so I decided to try and hone my own psychic abilities. My friend tried to teach me, but I did not have any success using his method. I couldn't even come close to getting any information from my spirit guides.

It was at that point that I ran across a kit that taught a technique on how to communicate with angels. I had been praying about my health for years and wondered if this would steer me in the right direction. Surely God's messengers would tell me what I needed to do to get well! Evidently, this was the path that I was supposed to take. Although angels and spirit guides work closely together, it must have been very important for me to connect with the angels!

Before my first session, I lit a candle and played the relaxing tape that was provided in the kit. I also put a few other things around me that made me feel good, including some beautiful crystals and my holy dirt from Chimayo. Well, now the stage was set for my divine communication and my spirituality soared. As I sat there quietly, the day's concerns and worries disappeared. This was my special time and I was going to make the most of it. I tried using the angel cards that came with the kit but got a little frustrated with them.

Eventually, I decided to try my hand at automatic writing. I was thinking that my hand would take off and move automatically but it did not. As a side note, this does happen for those who are not fearful of the divine process. I have since had a few experiences that were pretty amazing! I first wrote down a few questions that were on my mind. After each one, I began to write whatever thoughts popped into my head. At first I thought that I was just making up responses that I wanted to hear. Was this divine information or simply my imagination?

After I was healed, though, I reviewed all of my notes from that day. It seems that I was not only in communication with angels, but I had connected with my mother! There were many relevant responses to my questions from all of them, but there is one in particular that I would like to share with you. I wrote down the following question for my angels: "Will I be healed?" The next few words would reveal their answer and my future.

"In due time . . . in due time."

Chapter Five

I Can Hear Angels

Have you ever wondered about the mysteries in our world? Well, I certainly did and still do. I have always been intrigued by all things that couldn't be fully explained by the natural laws of science. That means that I was interested in a variety of subjects, including time travel, ghosts, UFO's, etc. Of course, I was always looking for some evidence as well. Yes, if you remember from a previous chapter, I'm the one who went on the hunt for a crop circle!

So, it is probably not much of a big surprise that some of my favorite television shows were Quantum Leap, the X-Files and Ghost Hunters. I didn't care too much for science fiction but the other paranormal stuff really intrigued me. The bigger the mystery, the better!

I always considered the definition of paranormal to be a little sketchy. It is considered to be anything that is outside the range of being normal and that cannot be fully explained by current scientific knowledge. But, what is "normal" for me may be totally different than what is "normal" for other folks. Likewise, what is "normal" here in our country may not be "normal" for someone in another country. So, to me, normal is a relative term.

"Current scientific knowledge" is also relative. At one point in history, "current scientific knowledge" convinced people that the world was flat. Thinking otherwise would have been considered absurd at that time. Well, those absurd "new age" thinkers proved everyone else to be wrong. Eventually, the accepted belief about the shape of the world changed.

There was also a point in time that "current scientific knowledge" would have declared space travel to be impossible and therefore, unbelievable. In 1865, Jules Verne wrote a futuristic science fiction book about traveling to the moon in a spacecraft. About 100 years later, we all know that this fictitious "paranormal" event became reality. As a side note, Verne even referred to a city in Florida as the launch site. Of course, this could take me into an entirely different topic about channeling and prophecies but I won't go there just yet. Perhaps in another book!

Anyway, I guess that some of you are wondering where I'm going with this. I am absolutely certain that there will be more areas in the paranormal field that will be recategorized as normal and generally accepted as real. So, keep an open mind to those subjects that might seem odd or weird to you right now. Just like space travel, those absurd and unusual ideas can become a new reality.

With that in mind, there are other areas of the paranormal field that I find quite fascinating. One of those areas involves the "sixth sense". Personally, I believe that God gave us a sixth sense or gut instinct as our own personal GPS to navigate through life. It is how He guides and communicates with us. All we have to do is pay attention so we don't miss the directions that He is providing.

How many times have you acted on your gut instinct and it turned out to be the correct choice for you? Did you have any data, facts, numbers, tangible evidence that would have led you to that decision? If it happens frequently, are you now defying the odds of scientific probability? Think about how you gained that information.

Now, there are folks who are very logical and science based in their way of thinking who don't completely understand what a sixth sense is. If they can't see it, it doesn't exist. But, many of these same people believe in a supreme being without being able to see this life form. Why is it such a stretch to believe that there is a sixth sense that was provided for us to stay in connection with Him?

A few years back, the term "sixth sense" was connected to a few other terms such as psychics, mediums, readings, ESP, telepathy, premonition, precognition, clairvoyance, etc. As the times have changed, New Age terms have been added such as intuitives, divination, ascended masters, channeling, etc. I think the terminology is changing for several reasons.

One is that there were many frauds in the early psychic fields that gave it a bad rap. There were also many good psychics but their information frightened people. They didn't connect the information to the divine world. But, society got some exposure and learned something about those gifts.

Another reason for the terminology shift is that we are learning where this information is coming from. I don't know what most people think, but I thought that there was a difference between the sources of information. I believed that psychics just grabbed information that was just floating out in the air. On the other hand, I thought that the New Agers were accessing divine information.

As I have since learned, the source is the same. It is all divine information and is delivered through God and His heavenly helpers. He has given us some wonderful guides in the spirit world to help us make our lives better. We have Jesus, angels, deceased relatives, and other esteemed people who once walked on earth to direct and teach us.

When you receive a reading, you are obtaining information from God or one of his helpers. These psychics, intuitives, or readers should be delivering information that will benefit you in some way. Many in this field are considered to be healers.

Unfortunately, many of us want to be dazzled with facts and figures to prove that the intuitive is genuine. It's really not a good idea to focus too much on the unimportant details. It would be better to pay attention to the overall message that they are telling you.

Now, like with any occupation, there are good psychics/readers and there are ones that don't know what they are doing. Don't let the few who are not genuine keep you from believing in all of them. It's like losing faith in all doctors because you had one bad experience. Most would just shop around until finding one that they like. But, I have digressed a bit here and need to get back on topic.

My favorite show around the time of my healing was Ghost Hunters. There were others on the air, but this one seemed more genuine and real to me. The show is about scientific investigations of places that have paranormal activity going on. In other words, they look for proof that ghosts exist. I think that due to our logicality, we want tangible evidence that the spirit world exists. I have heard on many occasion "I gotta see it to believe it". Well, evidence is now being gathered and I think that most people have become open to the possibility that ghosts do exist.

With that in mind, there is a lot of controversy over whether it is okay to investigate and disturb the spirits. I believe and have been told that it is appropriate to do so in order to learn more about them and their world. Communication with them can give us great peace of mind about our loved ones. God definitely wants us to know that heaven is a wonderful place and that our relatives are quite happy! This also helps us lessen our fear about death. If you think about it, communicating with the deceased can increase our spirituality and ultimately bring us closer to God.

Another controversial matter is whether we are going to connect with loved ones or something evil. Personally, I feel that if your intent is pure and you have asked for God's blessing, you will not have any problems. I have my own theories about negative spirits but it's a little complicated to explain here. I do believe that they can serve a useful purpose for those who have wandered off their path. Sometimes, a little concern is just enough to send people back in God's direction.

Anyway, I spent a lot of time watching ghost hunting shows and even bought a few books on the topic. I learned that I didn't need any fancy gadgets to pick up a ghost voice, but just an inexpensive digital recorder. Ghost voices are detected through something known as electronic voice phenomena or EVP. These sounds are usually heard as breaths or words on the recording that could not have been made by anything that was visible to the human eye. Although some are discounted as natural phenomena, many others are not.

It is theses "voices" that I found quite fascinating. Could we actually hear messages from beyond? Well, there is quite a lot of evidence that "something" is being recorded that cannot be seen. I truly believe that we are on the brink of scientifically proving that we can actually communicate with the deceased.

So, the ghost hunter in me, wanted to record my own EVP's. Two of my daughters worked at a local establishment that was purported to be haunted so off I went. Several people had reported some unusual phenomenon there that sounded paranormal. My daughter, Kim, actually caught a glimpse of a shadowy male figure wearing a cowboy hat. Now, many folks would assume that a "dark" figure would be considered to be negative in nature. I disagree completely. I think that this figure appeared in that particular form so that he could be seen. The establishment was a small smoky bar so if he had appeared any other way, no one would have seen him. They would have just thought it was cigarette smoke.

Anyway, Kim and I were very interested in making contact so we did several recorded sessions there. We wanted to see if the "Cowboy Man" needed any help. We couldn't hear much, but my oldest daughter, Amy, did hear her name on one of the recordings. I decided to download a free audio editing program to tweak it out and that is when the fun began!

It takes a special listening skill to discern a "voice" on a recording. To fine tune that skill, it is necessary to listen to the recording several times. It is also important to edit it in several different ways to see what works best. With that in mind, I spent many hours with headphones on. Eventually, I could pick up words and unusual sounds off of some of the recordings.

Around the same time, I felt a strong urge to visit my mother-in-law's grave. I rarely went out there so this was a little unusual for me. It was the same feeling that I got right after she had passed away. As mentioned earlier, that is when I visited my psychic friend, Donna. She was the one who told me that Barbara was trying to tell me something but I wouldn't slow down long enough to listen. I decided that this would be an ideal time to slow down and listen. I also decided that I could find out what she needed if I could just record her. So, I took my digital recorder out to the cemetery one afternoon in October of 2011.

It was too difficult for me to sit on the ground or stoop so I just stood by her headstone and began to talk to her. I recorded the session even though it was a windy day. I knew the wind would interfere but I hoped beyond hope that I would still be able to hear something on the recording. I had no idea at the time how this experience was a part of that divinely orchestrated healing that would soon take place.

I didn't spend too much time out there as I couldn't stand too long and I was getting sad. It had been nine years since she passed, but I still really missed that

I Can Hear Angels

woman. So, I got in my car, put my keys in the ignition and my mood immediately changed.

Well, it changed right after I realized that I had not said a prayer of protection before doing the recording. And that was unusual for me. I vaguely recalled reading somewhere that spirits can "jump" into your recorder if you don't ask for protection from God. Well, I don't think that is entirely true, but after that I covered my bases and asked for a blanket protection. And here's why...

After I got in the car, I felt like I wasn't alone. I wasn't entirely frightened but just felt a little apprehension. My general impression was that there were several very happy spirits in the back seat super excited about going on a road trip. Well, I wasn't sure if my mother-in-law was with them so I didn't ask anyone to leave. I now realize that they were super excited because of the role that they were about to play in my healing. As you read, you will understand more about what I mean. It is all about the chain of events and what it took for me to do certain things. In other words, it was in my best interest for them to tag along.

I know that their presence was very purposeful. It led me into memorizing a very comforting prayer that I would later use while in the hospital. I also learned some early lessons about the spirit world. Like I have said before, God has all kinds of helpers out there. And yes, some of them are ghosts.

So, anyway, I got distracted after arriving home and didn't think much more about them. I listened to my recording from the cemetery and was disappointed that I didn't hear anything unusual. All that I really heard was my pitiful sad voice and the wind. All of the sudden, I had a light bulb moment. I realized that Barbara's spirit wasn't out at that cemetery. Her spirit could be anywhere! After all, she had visited one of her grandchildren right after she passed away! I decided to just try and contact her from the comfort of my very own home.

The following day I sat on my stairs and proceeded to do a short recording session. I immediately listened to it and thought I heard someone tell me "Hi". Well, that surely got my curiosity up so I called my daughter Kim to come over and listen. My gut feeling told me that it was not Barbara. I really felt like it was my dad, who had passed away in 2006.

Kim immediately came over to see if she could "sense" anyone's presence and to listen to the recording. She had always "felt" things that could not be explained. In present terminology, she is considered to be a sensitive and could feel the presence of the spirit world. I didn't realize at the time how truly gifted she was. Not only could she feel them, but she could communicate with them as well.

Anyway, I really felt like someone was in my home because my dog, Bella, had been behaving strangely since my visit out to my mother-in-law's grave. I noticed that she appeared to be looking at something that I couldn't see and would occasionally bark and whine at it. This was unusual behavior for her.

I was a little confused, though, as I really felt like my dad was also there and he wasn't buried at that cemetery. I wanted some kind of confirmation so I did another session on the stairs with Kim. Was it just my dad who was with me? This would not have been the first time that he had visited us.

One of my granddaughters, Hailee, actually saw him a few months after he passed away. She was visiting me one afternoon and we were in the study. If memory serves me correct, Hailee was actually playing on the floor, near the doorway. She was about four years old and was just quietly entertaining herself. I was sitting on the couch and was also near the doorway. At some point, Hailee stopped what she was doing and looked down the hallway as if she saw something. It caught my attention so I looked down the hallway. Well, there was nothing there so I looked back at her. She had started to play again, but quickly stopped.

Now, here is where I got a little startled. She looked down the hallway again and shouted out "Boo!" Then I realized that her gaze was not at her eye level but much higher. I again looked down the hallway towards the stairs and saw nothing. I really felt like she saw someone so I asked her about it. I didn't feed her any information but just asked her who she saw. She replied "Santa Claus" which puzzled me at the time. Later, I realized who it was. The only man that I knew that would have fit that description was my father. He didn't have a white beard but he was a rather portly man and the timing made sense to me. He had just passed away.

So, getting back to my story . . . Kim and I finished up another recording on the stairs and tried our best to help any spirits that were still at my house. I felt very strongly that there was more than one present and was concerned that some of them might be stuck in our world.

Well, we didn't know exactly how it all worked, but we were going to make sure we did our best to help them. We proceeded to tell the non-family spirits that they could not stay at my house and that they should go on in to heaven. We also told the family members that they were allowed to stay. Our session was closed with the Lord's Prayer and we believed that all was well.

A few days later, I did another recording on the stairs as I was still trying to get answers from my family. I assumed that it would be easier to hear them since we had asked everyone else to leave. I had heard all kinds of sounds and words on the recordings but nothing definitive about who made them.

At this point, I asked my house guests to talk a little louder as I wanted to be able to hear them over the ringing in my ears. Now many people know that ringing in the ears is considered a medical condition called tinnitus. I will take this opportunity to point out that it can also be a prelude to the divine gift of clairaudience and not to be alarmed about it.

Well, over the next few days, I had some strange experiences. There were a few times that I felt like someone whispered in my ear and this startled me. I also felt like someone touched me. I wasn't sure who it was but I considered just asking everyone to leave. I didn't do this, though, as I still wanted to talk to my family.

Instead, I again asked God to protect my family and I set down the house rules. The rules were that no one could whisper in my ear or touch me again. At that time, I wasn't ready for that type of communication. I also told them that they were not to enter my bedroom or my study. I didn't mind feeling their presence, but I needed my private space.

I also felt like there were still spirits that needed to move on and I wanted to help. I believed at this point that they were leaving messages for me on the recordings. I asked Kim to come over so we could do a crossing over ceremony. Although we had done an informal one before, we decided to make it more formal. We sat facing the stairs and recorded this session as well. We both felt like the stairway and upper landing was their gateway to heaven. In retrospect, this is the same area that Hailee had seen my dad.

We began with a prayer of blessing and protection from God. At this point, we also called in other divine beings that would like to assist in the crossing. I think this was the first time that I requested guardian angels for their assistance. Interestingly, this is the first recording where unusual tinkling sounds are evident.

We began to talk to these spirits as if they were living, trying to convince them to go into heaven. I really don't know whether we actually assisted in crossing anyone over or if the ceremony provided lessons for us. Through this process, though, I did completely memorize the Lord's Prayer. It came in very handy about three weeks later. Either way, it was an amazing experience.

What is interesting is that I continued to feel like someone was touching me. I couldn't figure out who didn't cross over. Well, I know now that a touch from the spirit world doesn't mean that they aren't in heaven. This could have been one of my friendly ghosts from the cemetery assisting in my miracle process. I know that the communication from the spirit world was important for me. Any contact from that world was quite necessary for my future and there was never any danger to me. I had always lived my life in the manner that God wanted me to so I know that I was always protected.

After reviewing the recording from the last crossing over session, I realized that I might be communicating with beings other than ghosts. According to everything that I had studied, ghosts can only make brief sounds on recordings as they don't have much energy. I had watched many different ghost hunting shows and they rarely came up with more than one or two words from their investigations.

But, on my recordings, I was hearing something else. I was hearing unusual tinkling sounds that were very melodic and seemed to respond to my questions. A few other people could hear them but some simply dismissed them as my wind chimes. I remember occasionally hearing the wind chimes myself during the recording as it was a little breezy. If it had been really windy, though, I would have stopped my recording and taken them down. By then, I knew what caused interference and had eliminated all of the other noise factors around the house.

I was also hearing strings of words and even full sentences. I once clearly heard someone say "Bella's barking" in a very sweet and clear voice. Well, that made perfect sense as I could hear her bark on the recording. But who said it and why was it so clear? I remember thinking "Was this a ghost? A spirit guide? AN ANGEL?

It was during this time that I was so engaged in these recordings that I almost forgot that I was sick. Those lilting musical sounds were simply fascinating to me and I was enjoying every minute of this research! By the 26th of October, 2011, I believed that I was hearing either spirit guides or angels on these recordings! It was right about that time that I had quite an interesting and life altering experience.

I finished up my research on one of the recent recordings and took my headphones off. I got a little alarmed as I could still hear a slight buzzing and ringing in my ears. I thought I might have had the volume up too loud and damaged my eardrums. After awhile, I realized that this was simply not the case. I was now hearing musical sounding words and partial sentences without listening to any recording!

At that time, I was puzzled so I picked up the phone and called my friend, Donna. She was well versed in everything paranormal so I figured that she could help. I explained what I was hearing and she simply told me that I had turned on my "third eye" and I was now clairaudient. I had heard the term "third eye" before and knew that it was a spiritual term. It is considered to be your gateway to a higher consciousness. Well, that was fine but what the heck did clairaudient mean? Well, we got off the phone and I got on the computer.

I found out that clairaudience is defined as having the ability to hear sounds that are outside the scope of ordinary experience. It is commonly referred to as the "divine ear" and considered to be a gift from God. At that time, I couldn't find too much about it on the internet but I did find a few interesting articles.

One article was about Joan of Arc and her extraordinary clairaudient gift. According to what I read, she began hearing the voices of saints and angels when she was about thirteen years old. They guided her and within three years she was leading the French army in successful military campaigns!

Although she was later convicted of heresy and burned at the stake I feel very strongly that her role in history was very important. I don't know all of the details as I haven't completely studied her life. But, God would have known what would happen to her and would not have guided her into that particular life if it wasn't necessary. Eventually, she was canonized and has become known as St. Joan of Arc.

Another article referred to the many instances in the Bible where voices from the divine were heard. One in particular is when the angels announced the birth of Jesus to the shepherds. There are also other supernatural cases reported in the bible where people heard the voice of God talking to them. These are all examples of clairaudience, where ordinary people hear supernatural voices.

As far as I know, most of these cases are generally accepted to be a real part of our history and are directly linked to God. With that in mind, I wonder why so many in our day consider "hearing voices" to be a sign of mental illness? Shouldn't the final discernment be in determining what those voices are saying? When did we lose our faith about how He communicates?

I will admit that in the beginning stages of my clairaudient gift I was a little unsure of to whom I was talking with. My logical self thought that I might be hearing ghost voices. I also pondered over the idea that a new electronic device was emitting frequencies that I could actually hear in my head. I remember wondering who was in my neighborhood sending out electronic signals that I could pick up. Okay, don't laugh. Isn't that similar to how a dog whistle works?

Anyway, about that time, I heard these voices talking about something that was going on inside my home. Well, that ruled out my electronic gadget theory. I couldn't make out everything that was being said, but I kept listening. It was if there were many people talking at the same time and I could only catch a few words and phrases. It's kind of like listening to the television or radio from another room. You can occasionally make out a word or two but you can't hear the whole conversation.

At some point I began hearing musical instruments. I don't remember what I heard first, but I did hear organ music and a harp. Well, that did it for me! When I hear harps, I think of angels! The realization simply astounded me. These were angels communicating with me! I kept thinking to myself, angels? Really? I can hear angels? You mean those heavenly beings that work for GOD are talking to me?

I can only imagine that my angels were ready to hit me over the head to convince me that it was them. Instead, they were very patient and let me just process everything that was going on. I believe that they knew the harp music was the only way I would be convinced about the origins of this communication.

So, as the days went by, I began to try and fine tune this new gift. It was still difficult to understand them without having ambient noise around me. In order to hear them better, I focused on the sounds that were around me such as the humming of the refrigerator, computer or any type of fan. These all produce what is known as "white noise" which can be very beneficial for the body and the brain. I won't go in to much detail here but I know that among other things, it forced me to sit quietly, relax and meditate.

At this point, I was hearing a lot of musical sounds and I did hear my name quite often. First, middle, maiden and last. And sometimes, in various orders. The words I heard were always repetitive and I could occasionally understand sentences. I realize now that there was a reason for me not to hear them very well, but I'll get in to that a little later.

On one occasion, though, I did ask them if they could sing to me in a Gregorian sounding chant. You might think this is an odd request but I had once heard a fellow singing in this manner in a stairwell. Because of the acoustics there, it sounded as if it was in a church environment. It gave me such a spiritual feeling that I wanted to hear it again. I remember sitting next to the fan by my bed and listening intently to see if my request would be answered. The next thing you know I could hear the same melody and it was absolutely amazing!

I had another awesome experience while listening to that fan. I was just waking up and had not even opened my eyes yet. Suddenly, I realized that I was hearing music and my clock radio was not on. Much to my surprise, I recognized the tune as "You Are My Sunshine!" Those amazing voices were singing to me in perfect harmony and I was overjoyed! It was such a wonderful way to wake up!

As the days went by, I continued to listen to their voices and began to spend more time outdoors and relaxing. That is where I felt the closest to God and my angels. I began to study everything around me and noticed details like I had never seen before. Among other things, I began to notice the movement of the trees when the wind blew. And I listened to them.

Embedded within the rustling of those trees I could hear their voices; beautiful, spiritual voices. And they were talking to me! Tears streamed down my face as the reality of this all sank in. I was hearing God's angels! I had never felt that kind of spiritual connection! As I listened to the trees, I thought about my Cherokee ancestors. I realized at that moment that this must have been how they communicated with the divine world.

I thought my husband would enjoy hearing about this wonderful experience so I decided to share it with him. He knew that I could hear "something" and I really wanted to make sure that he knew how spiritual it was. As soon as I opened my mouth, I realized what it sounded like. I was only a few weeks into my experience with this new gift so I had not forgotten how most people feel about hearing voices. I kept trying to explain how phenomenal it was but my story wasn't going over very well.

I decided not to let this bother me and just enjoy my new gift. I found that every day was like a new adventure and I felt really special. On top of that, I was happy! Really happy! Happier than I had ever been in my entire life! I don't even remember feeling like I was handicapped, although I certainly still was.

Among other things, mobility had become a big problem for me. It had even become necessary for me to ride in the motorized scooters when I was out shopping. But, I was so happy that even having to ride in them didn't bother me like it had before.

As a matter of fact, I even had a really cool experience one day while riding in one of those scooters. I was just cruising around and doing my shopping when I heard my name called. Now, most of the time the voices that I heard sounded fairly faint and from within my head. But this voice was very loud and different. It seemed to originate from the loudspeaker. Yes, I could actually hear my angels talking to me through the store's public address system!

At first I was a little startled and I looked around to see if anyone else could hear them. Then, I realized that it was just for me and I smiled. This experience taught me a very valuable lesson that I understood much later. It proved to me that they could be very loud when necessary and it really didn't have much to do with my skill level. On that note, I would love to share the humorous story about "Clean up on Aisle Nine" but I'll save that one for another time.

For about four weeks, I practiced my newfound gift of Angel Talk. I was still having difficulty in understanding everything that they said so I did several things. I continued to spend more time outdoors and listening to ambient noise. This in turn, forced me into full meditation mode. I know that the meditation not only benefited me in a spiritual manner, but had positive physiological effects on my body. I also spent more time using my digital recorder to try and understand their messages. I could actually understand them better on the recordings.

At that time, I also still felt like there were spirits present at my home that were trying to tell me something. I wasn't sure how to help them and I really wanted to get them out of my house. I believed that my angels would help mc if I could understand their messages. I was also very much interested in proving that my angels were real by recording a message that others could hear.

It may sound a tad bit confusing, but it was really quite simple. I believed I was hearing ghosts that needed my help; I believed that my angels would tell me how to help them; and I was looking for proof that it was all real so my family would not think I was crazy.

Well, that's not exactly what happened. Although my daughter, Kim, believed that there was something very spiritual going on, others did not. Namely, my husband. He thought I was getting a little too obsessed with the whole thing because I spent a lot of time with headphones on. I think he was starting to doubt my sanity. I didn't realize at the time, that this was probably necessary during the course of my healing.

Anyway, I was hearing a lot of intriguing messages on those recordings. That's when the Nancy Drew in me came out and I wanted to solve this mystery. I have always been more of a night owl so this was my best time to do research.

Now, this is where things get a little fuzzy so I'll do my best to recreate what happened next. I may have adjusted my nighttime medication since I was up so late or I may have completely missed it. This was a benzodiazepine so I was always very careful about adjusting the dosage. In all reality, I may have missed another medication as well.

After a few nights of staying up until the wee hours of the morning, I began to feel unwell. Actually, I began experiencing chest pain early one morning that I believed was from a potential heart attack. I asked my angels if I should go to the hospital and they said "Yes, but not to worry." I wasn't real concerned, but I woke my husband up. He drove me out to the emergency room and that is when the fun began.

I am being a tad bit facetious here as I was in for a very rough time. But, as you read along, you will see that it was well worth it. At some point during the next eleven days, God performed one of His amazing miracles on me.

Chapter Six

The Miracle

A miracle is commonly described as an extraordinary event believed to be created through supernatural powers. It can be in direct contradiction to known scientific law or can occur through created nature. Miracles can be delivered in all kinds of packages. Sometimes the package is so small that we don't even see it. I believe that they are much more common than most people think.

Miracles that defy scientific law are considered the most dramatic and impressive of them all. Those that occur from created nature are also quite extraordinary but may be less understood as to be divine in origin. By created nature, I mean where God sets things in motion and these events can be explained through science. He also oversees the process. One example is where people pray for rain and it subsequently rains.

Miracles of physical healing can also occur by either of the methods explained above. I believe that in November, 2011, I experienced both kinds of this extraordinary divine intervention! I'm convinced that there was a divine touch that halted my genetic disorder during my hospital stay. I don't know how but perhaps my DNA was changed or a faulty switch was somehow turned off. After that touch, I believe that a natural chain of events occurred that were orchestrated and overseen by supernatural beings. The end result for me was an absolutely amazing healing!

Of course, I didn't realize what was going on at the time and certainly didn't think it was amazing. On the contrary, it was quite a traumatic experience. I spent about eleven days in the hospital over a course of two weeks. It was so traumatic that one of the major delays in writing this book was my inability to do the research necessary for this particular chapter. I realize now that I was suffering from "post traumatic stress disorder" which my angels helped me to work through. But, alas, there were many lessons that were learned and perhaps the delay was necessary.

It is very possible that this whole experience was simply a part of the plan that my soul chose before entering this life. I believe that we are born with a predetermined path but it can change according to our free will. I like to think that we are all here on earth to do good and make a positive difference in this world. Some get off their paths, though, because of free will. This means that they can make their lives better or worse. Among other things, they can have a longer life span than what was originally planned or a shorter one. I believe that there is no predetermined destiny that cannot be altered. If that were the case, why would anyone strive to live a better life? Well, we are getting pretty deep here, so let's get back to the story. I could go on but my angels told me to save it for a later time.

So, during my healing, I visited three hospitals and was admitted to two of them. Some of you are probably wondering why three hospitals but I'll explain about that later. I'm not completely sure what I gained from each one of them but I have often thought that the number three is a powerful number. For those of you interested in numerology, the number eleven keeps appearing in my story as well. I believe that there is a lot of legitimacy to numbers and numerology as being significant in our lives, so keep an open mind!

With all of that in mind, I'll now share the details on how God and His heavenly beings worked to heal me. To keep myself and everyone else from being too confused, I decided to break down what happened to me by each hospital. I think you will find this quite interesting!

Hospital #1

As I mentioned in the previous chapter, I woke up one morning experiencing chest pain. I was also experiencing some shortness of breath and felt dizzy. My angels told me that everything was fine, but I should go to the hospital. I wasn't particularly frightened about anything, but wanted to make sure that everything was okay.

I don't quite remember too much about the emergency room so most of this information was gleaned from my records. After arriving, I had an EKG that was considered borderline. They monitored me for cardiac problems and ran some other tests. My liver function tests came back slightly low but everything else was fairly normal.

I also had a chest x-ray done that did not show any evidence of cardiopulmonary disease. What it did show was that I had what is considered a slight collapsing of both lungs. The collapsing can be caused by various problems, including shallow breathing and pulmonary embolism. The condition creates an oxygen deficit which causes shortness of breath. It takes time to heal

The Miracle

but can be done so through deep breathing exercises, and movement. Basically, you just re-inflate the lungs.

The chest x-ray also showed fibrosis which is considered scar tissue. This can be caused by several factors, one of those being a side effect of a medication that I had started back in 2009. I can't say for sure that the medication was the problem, but there were many other problems that popped up after I began that particular prescription. I don't believe that they were all coincidental. This medication was also a big problem for me during my hospital stays which I'll get in to a little later in this chapter.

Anyway, I am going in to great detail about the chest x-ray for several reasons. One is because the collapsing, which "takes time to heal" had completely resolved by a second chest x-ray that was done just eight days later. And the fibrosis which is considered to be permanent scarring? COMPLETELY GONE. Intrigued? Keep reading.

Now, my recollection of being in the emergency room is strangely missing from my memory bank. I am going to blame this on the fact that I started having seizures during my stay there. They were considered "passing out" spells but I know now that they were a type of seizure. You see, as the hours ticked by in the emergency room, I was getting further behind in my dose of several prescriptions, including the medication that I mentioned earlier. That medication is the most commonly prescribed drug for fibromyalgia and is classified as an anticonvulsant (a seizure medication).

Needless to say, I was admitted to the hospital and transferred up to a room. This would be one of many rooms that I would experience my healing in. One of those, I shall call the "mystery room" as I cannot quite place it in my timeline. More on that later!

By that evening, my glucose became elevated, my blood gases were off and my oxygen saturation level was at 96%. I had a CT scan and an MRI and neither indicated a cause for seizure activity. Another EKG was done and it was also considered borderline normal. Then an echocardiogram was ordered.

I found the results of this echocardiogram (echo) to be quite perplexing. It had been noted on a previous echo from a few years back that I had two slightly leaky valves; namely the mitral and tricuspid valve. It was also noted that there was mild calcification around the mitral valve. This most recent echo showed only one valve leaking and it was the pulmonic valve. From what I have read, the valves don't repair themselves. Even if they do, it seemed rather unusual to me. And the calcification on the mitral valve? It was completely gone. In light of everything else that has happened to me, I find this very significant.

So back to my story. I have very little recollection about my first day in the hospital. The second day was a little different. For all of you numerologists, I will take this opportunity to point out that date. It was November 11, 2011 which is also 11-11-11. A friend of mine who is a great medium told me that this was a significant date for angel presence and I'd have to agree with him. With that in mind, I found something else rather intriguing. Out of the few handwritten notes on my progress records, one of them was entered at 11:11am on 11-11-11. This was when my cardiologist signed off from my case.

To further add to the mystery of numbers, there are other elevens in my story. I was actually born on the 11th of October. And, my husband's family lived on an 11th Avenue for many years. This was the same house where our entire family had many celebrations with my mother-in-law, Barbara. Yes, the same person that I feel was very important in my healing! I'll bet you can't guess what their entire address was. Yes, it was 111-11th Avenue!

Anyway, by the morning of my second day in the hospital, my oxygen saturation dropped down to 94% and my body temperature was recorded as 96.7. My glucose was slightly elevated and my electrolyte levels were abnormal. Liver and kidney blood tests were slightly abnormal and I was nauseated and vomiting. I felt like every time I fell asleep that I quit breathing. It was like I had sleep apnea and I was frightened about it. In retrospect, this could have been a problem as people with neuromuscular disease can experience sleep disordered breathing. Medications can further exacerbate this problem.

It was noted on my chart that I was experiencing impaired cardiac and respiratory function and still having some type of "passing out" episodes. They were not completely recognized as seizures since I didn't exhibit the signs of the most common type of seizure, the grand mal. It was also noted in my chart that I was hallucinating and considered to be psychotic.

At this point, no one but my family recognized that this was a medication withdrawal. My husband believed it was a withdrawal from a benzodiazepine that I may have missed but the doctors disagreed. They were still administering it to me. No one realized that the real culprit was the seizure medication. In their defense, there is very little literature about the horrendous side effects of that particular drug. This would include dangerous and life threatening repercussions from a "cold turkey" withdrawal, which is what I was going through.

So, word to the wise: avoid prescription medications if at all possible. The literature that is published to warn of side effects is not always reliable. Studies that are done to ensure that the drug is safe are very limited. Some of those studies can even be fabricated, as in some of the studies that were associated with the medication that I took. Yes, I said fabricated which means they were made up studies. Also, there are many times that the dangerous side effects of some of these prescriptions don't surface until many people become ill or die. Even then, the association to the drug can be difficult to prove. To complicate matters, some people never report their adverse effects to the FDA.

I don't mean to frighten you about this, but please be cautious. A few years back I probably would not have said this, but if you are worried about your prescriptions, just pray about it. Do your part and God will take care of the rest. When you ask Him for help, he sends in his very finest to make sure that your needs are met. On that note, I'll continue.

Angel Talk

During those first few days in the hospital, I prayed almost non-stop. I didn't know many prayers but my angels had just recently helped me completely learn the Lord's Prayer (remember those crossings?) And boy did that come in handy. I was frightened and it gave me peace of mind. It also kept that same mind very busy so I didn't focus on the fear.

My angels also kept my mind busy by singing songs to me. Some of them were nursery rhymes that I had to retrieve out of my memory bank. They also stimulated my thought process in ways that I don't even understand. I watched the clock doing simple math calculations and everything became a mystery. They encouraged me to analyze details about everything that was going on around me. I guess this could have been just to keep me busy but I feel like they were helping me work on cognitive rehabilitation. You see, that medication that I keep talking about had left me with a very big brain fog. And perhaps it was the cause of the "hyperintensities" that showed up in my MRI.

My angels also monitored my sleep schedule. Sometimes they encouraged me to sleep and sometimes they encouraged me to stay awake. I don't know what was going on but I have to wonder if they weren't acting like those sleep apnea alarm bells.

The Miracle

Even though my angels kept reassuring me that I was going to be okay, I believed at one point that I might die from this ordeal. I decided at that point to tell my kiddos goodbye. I wanted to let them know how special each one of them was and that I loved them. Obviously, none of them took that very well. I didn't realize that this would upset them so much or I probably wouldn't have said anything. But, I'm one of those people that likes to cover their bases.

They were so upset with what I said that they decided to take action. Besides reassuring me that I was going to be fine, they decided to phone a friend to lead a formal prayer session. It was my friend, Donna, who lived out of state at the time. I don't completely understand the significance of all this but believe there were many purposes. I believe that their worries were somewhat eased and that they began to pray more.

I also remember my angels advising me as to when I needed to eat and drink. I had absolutely no appetite and I really didn't want anything. I had been having episodes of nausea, vomiting and diarrhea so that doesn't surprise me. When my stomach settled down a bit, though, I did manage to get some nourishment in. Just enough to keep everyone happy. The bright side of this is that I did lose a few pounds while being hospitalized.

My angels also reminded me when it was time to urinate. There was one occasion when I was so out of it that I didn't realize that my bladder was full. In retrospect, I think it was in a major spasm. I couldn't get up to go to the toilet and they kept encouraging me to just release it in the bed. I suddenly realized how painful it was and tried and tried to just let it go. I wasn't having any luck until I actually "saw" them jumping on it. Now, by that I mean that I "saw" them in my mind's eye. Not sure if it was just a suggestion or actual pressure was applied, but it certainly worked!

I also remember moving around in the bed quite a bit. Now, most bystanders would say that I was psychotic and thrashing around. But, I would say that I was following instructions and moving constantly. Not instructions from the medical staff, but more instructions from my angel buddies. It's important to remember that sometimes it is all about perspective.

At this point, they were calmly giving me precise and detailed directions on how and when to move. I was encouraged to roll from side to side for as long as I could and I did just that. I don't remember if they told me or I just "felt" it but I believed that I had a blood clot. It motivated me just enough to keep following their orders. As you read, you will understand that this was a real possibility.

I also bolted up in bed on occasion which drove my husband batty. I distinctly remember him trying to hold me down; and I mean trying. I can only speculate as to how I got the strength, but I kept him from stopping my movement. According to my husband, I even lifted him off of me! Now go figure that one out and don't forget that I had a muscle disorder!

During those first few days, my angels also instructed me to do unusual maneuvers. There were times when they had me lay on one side or the other and hold my breath. On two occasions I distinctly remember feeling a "pop" and thought a blood clot was moving through my heart. Now I don't necessarily believe it was a blood clot, but I felt a similar feeling after I got home. I believe it was related to either my heart or my lungs. Either way, I have no doubt that they were helping me resolve some issue.

Now, here's where I'd like to throw out some explanations for what happened. During movement, certain things happen within the body. I'm being simplistic as I'm not a doctor but here it goes. Movement speeds up the metabolism which has multiple benefits. Increased metabolism likely cleared certain medications out of my body quicker. I also had a thyroid problem so I believe that it was affected as well. Movement also warms the body up and my body temperature was dropping. A rise in body temperature warms the blood up and that would have aided in keeping my blood thinner or dissolving any clots that were forming.

Movement also exercises the muscles and mine were in a weakened condition. I was not only encouraged to move back and forth in the bed but to grip the sides of the bed and lift my body up. Occasionally, I did bolt up and tried to get out of bed. Not sure if this was part of the exercise plan or if it was behavior resulting from the drug withdrawal.

I'm guessing that part of that behavior was from the medication withdrawal and I believe that my angels protected me on several occasions. I kept hearing them say "left side down" so I always leaned to the left when I was about to fall over. That training made a huge difference on one particular occasion when I tried to get out of bed. I immediately felt myself falling to the ground and leaned to the left. I hit the ground fairly hard but completely protected my right elbow, which was already injured. I'll share with you in a later chapter how they completely rehabilitated that elbow without me even knowing it!

Although I protected my right elbow, I did unfortunately rip out my IV in the fall. What's interesting is that I didn't feel a lick of pain. Nada. I

The Miracle

just looked at it and could hear everyone making a fuss. The hospital's rapid response team promptly rushed in to make sure that everything was okay. I'm not sure who took care of me but there was an "Angel" among the nurses. No, silly, not a real angel. I mean there was a nurse with the name "Angel". Yes, I found that quite interesting, myself.

About thirty minutes after that, I had another episode. Evidently, I wasn't feeling too well and had been complaining about a headache and visual disturbances prior to the first fall. During the second episode, I completely lost consciousness and they performed what's known as a "sternum rub". I have heard that these are pretty painful if you are awake. Evidently, I wasn't.

It was after this that they decided to move me to another room with a sitter. I believe it was in that room that my behavior got a little worse. I remember a few things that were.. . . . let's just say . . . very unusual for me. I'm embarrassed to say that I even tried to bite a nurse. Well, I was frightened and thought that she was going to hurt me. Hopefully, she is reading this book and will accept my apology. You might say that I wasn't at my best that day.

I also remember crying and yelling out for my family but to no avail. I was petrified and wanted them to stay with me. They were the only ones that knew what my medication sensitivities were. Not only did I once code on morphine, but I almost died another time from taking an antibiotic. No, I'm not exaggerating. A blood sugar reading in the teens is very dangerous.

I knew that my body didn't process medications like most people. That is why I kept refusing any medications that were new for me. But, because of my behavior, I had lost credibility with the staff. I knew that they would not believe anything I said and I felt like I was at their mercy. I didn't realize that this just wasn't the case at all.

I remember having a conversation with my angels around that time as they knew how frightened and upset I was. During that particular conversation I said to them, "What if they give me a medication that I can't have?" Their response was very simple and to the point. They replied, "Cathy . . . just remember who is in charge."

My eyes are welling up with tears as I type this as it was an amazing epiphany for me. There I was, lying in a hospital bed and I had absolutely no control over anything that was going on around me. I was too sick to leave; no one believed anything that I said; and my family was not allowed to stay with me. That is

The Miracle

where I learned a valuable lesson. I had to let go of all my fears and turn everything over to God. There was nothing that I could do about the situation and I needed to relax. Perhaps this is exactly what I needed to get out of my logical mind and trust Him. I didn't completely understand the lesson at the time but the process had been started. The incident now also serves as a good story for others to learn the same lesson.

During my entire hospital stay I was also upset that most of the staff didn't recognize the seizures. I knew that they believed that I was just faking them. I had been there almost five days before my neurologist diagnosed me with a seizure disorder. I'm not sure what clouded their judgment but feel it must have been necessary for my healing that they missed it. I have since learned what I believe is the type of seizure that I was experiencing. It is called a partial or focal seizure.

A partial seizure occurs when only a limited area of the brain is affected by abnormal electrical disturbances. Symptoms can vary according to where in the brain the disturbance is located. People with these types of seizures may not lose consciousness and may or may not be aware of the events that occur at the time. They may also have periods of time lost from memory and have staring spells. The seizure can also affect just one side of the body. There are many other symptoms but those are the ones that I can directly associate with what happened with me. I also distinctly remember my angels repeatedly telling me "seizure disorder". Of course, they also repeatedly told me that I was going to be just fine.

There was one occasion where I remember zoning out right after sitting up in bed. One of my visitors looked me straight in the eye and said, "Yes, lights are on but nobody's home". I have to say that it was an unusual feeling to not be able to interact or respond. I was normally a very talkative person. My nickname isn't "Chatty Cathy" for nothing!

So, during the course of my stay at this particular hospital I was moved around several times. I tried to place each room with events that I could remember, but one room in particular has been elusive. It may have been a legitimate room and in my records but I can't make the sequence of events make sense. At any rate, I shall call this room the "Mystery Room".

From what I recall, this room was smaller than the others and seemed to be a private one. It was quiet and darker than the others, as if there were no windows. There was a lady in the room who I suppose was keeping watch over me. I distinctly remember that she was wearing regular street clothes and not scrubs. She was a black woman and I think she was a little heavyset.

I believe it was in this room that I spoke with Jesus. I distinctly remember feeling His presence in the upper left side of the room. I don't remember much about the visit but definitely remember His question. He asked me, "Are you ready to go?" I became a little concerned that I was getting ready to die and I really wasn't ready to go. I responded, "No" but He repeated the question. I gave Him the same response, unsure as to what it all meant.

I must have been concerned that I was going to die as I asked the sitter to pray for me. Now here is where it gets interesting. She opened the cabinet above a desk area and pulled out some kind of oil. She prayed for me and applied this oil to my forehead in the shape of a cross.

Now, I can only speculate as to the meaning of this, but I somehow think that I got baptized or received a holy blessing of some type. I don't believe that I had a choice to live or die as Jesus and God knew my purpose. They also would have known what was in my heart. At present, the only reason I can come up with for the question is that it created an action on my part. My angels are leaving this one for me to ponder over and I feel sure that the answer will be revealed at some point in the future.

So after five and a half days of being hospitalized, I decided that I was ready to leave. They weren't quite ready to release me as they wanted to do a sleep study on me. But, I was afraid to stay and thought I was stable enough to go home and finish recuperating. Well, I was wrong about that one.

<u>Hospital #2</u>

I had only been home one full day when I received an unsettling phone call. It was a cousin's husband informing me about her death. I wasn't sure why he called me as I had not met either one of them. I had only talked with her one time on the phone when we had discussed getting together. I found out that she was disabled, too and had difficulty getting around. I had been really excited about meeting her as she was also interested in our family genealogy. But, because of my ongoing fatigue, I didn't make the plan to go. She was about an hour's drive away and I knew that I would need someone to go with me.

Anyway, I got off the phone and became very upset. I think this is where my guilt kicked in as I remember her husband kindly saying "She really wanted to meet you." He also spoke about some family pictures that I might be interested in and I felt the need to go see him. I got his information and told him that I was on my way. Well, that's not what happened.

I asked my husband to take me and I began to get ready. As I walked through my house, I began dragging one of my legs and feeling out of sorts. I thought I may have been having a stroke, so I asked to be taken to the hospital. This time, I wanted to go to the one where my own doctors could treat me so we drove thirty minutes to Galveston. I remained conscious during the drive but knew that something was majorly wrong. I could barely talk and didn't have complete control over my body. My glasses slid off of my face and I couldn't stop them. I remember being annoyed as I figured that they were scratched (and that they were). The drive seemed to take an eternity and I felt a sense of urgency.

We finally arrived at the emergency room and someone opened my door. I tried to get out and promptly collapsed. I just couldn't make my arms and legs move like I wanted them to. I didn't realize at the time that this was another seizure. This would make sense as I don't remember quite a bit of what happened. Evidently, I had a CT scan done of my brain but have no recollection of it.

What I do remember is seeing my own doctor for the first time since this ordeal. I can't tell you how relieved I was to see his face! Of course, I don't think he felt the same way about seeing me. I remember thinking that I must have really looked bad. He entered the room and I thought he was going to fall to his knees.

Well, he was probably just stooping down to sit in the little chair beside my bed, but that wasn't my impression at the time. I'm sure I looked a complete mess. I was scared out of my mind and I'm sure he could see it. I grabbed his hand and didn't want to let go. I finally felt like someone that knew my case would take appropriate care of me. He recognized my condition of a drug withdrawal and recommended a facility for me to go to. They had a facility within that medical complex but he didn't think it was a good fit for me.

Personally, I think it was part of the divine process for me to not be treated within that facility. They had all of my medical records and could have potentially put me back on the medication that God was trying to get me off of. As a matter of fact, my neuromuscular specialist worked at the same facility and I feel sure that he would have known what was going on. Perhaps, it wasn't by chance that he was unavailable during my ordeal. I had unsuccessfully tried to contact him while I was in the first hospital. I don't believe in coincidences.

The Miracle

So, I was released from the emergency room and off we went. The only problem was that I recognized the place that we were going as a psychiatric facility. Evidently, they also treated drug withdrawal cases. When we arrived, my anxiety level quadrupled. I tried to remain calm while I believed that my worst nightmare was about to come true. I had always feared that someone would doubt my sanity and lock me up.

I pulled myself together and went along to be triaged. I found the atmosphere in this place to be absolutely depressing and the staff was slightly short of being friendly. I noticed that the rooms were not private and I somehow felt that I was in danger. I told my husband that I felt like I would be raped if I stayed there and asked him to take me home. I told him that I would help him research another facility that I felt was more appropriate to meet my needs.

Fortunately, one of the assessment clerks said that they didn't handle withdrawals from the benzodiazepine that they thought I was withdrawing from. That cinched up my release so we went home. I spent one day at home trying to figure out what to do when I experienced another episode.

Hospital #3

On November 19th, I again woke up with chest pains. I was still having some major sleep issues and felt like I wasn't breathing properly. My angels told me to wake up my husband and this didn't go over very well with him. He was emotionally exhausted from everything that had been going on and was very short-tempered with me.

Now, I was in a dilemma. My husband wouldn't take me to the hospital and my angels said that I needed to go. They told me to call an ambulance and that is exactly what I did. Evidently, there was some legitimacy to my problem as I spent the next five days in the cardiac care unit of Hospital #3.

My EKG in the emergency room was abnormal, although my oxygen saturation rate had improved to near 100%. I can only speculate here, but feel sure that it was because my lungs had re-inflated. Mysteriously, they were now normal on my chest x-ray. Perhaps all of those angel-guided breathing exercises and movement in Hospital #1 re-inflated my lungs. My only question is what happened to the fibrosis that showed up on the x-ray from several days earlier? As I mentioned earlier, it was now gone.

To further add to the mystery, I had several other tests run that evening including one called a D-Dimer test. This is a test to determine how well your blood clotting system is running. Mine was extremely elevated which can be indicative that the body has dissolved a clot. Well, maybe those angels of mine were telling me the truth about that blood clot from the first hospital. It is very possible that I had one before I ever entered Hospital #1. Here again, blood clots can be a side effect of the medication that I was withdrawing from.

I began to feel much safer during my stay at this hospital. I was still battling this feeling that I wasn't breathing when I fell asleep but it had improved. I also felt like I was short of breath but this hospital treated me accordingly. It was here that I finally received respiratory treatment and this made me feel better.

Although the worst of the withdrawal was over, anxiety was still an issue. It was at this point that I had another visit from Jesus. Yes, Jesus came to visit me again! I heard His now familiar voice instructing me on how to deal with the anxiety. He sang a very rhythmic song, much like what a rap song would sound like. I was also instructed to gently rock along with the rhythm and this would relax me. I immediately relaxed and drifted off to sleep! I woke back up and shared this wonderful piece of information with my husband. I told him that Jesus had just visited me and taught me how to relax!

My husband promptly ran out of the room and I just began my relaxation therapy again. I thought he was going to share the good news with the nurses but he probably was going to report me as hallucinating. I don't know if anyone came back in with him as I was fast asleep.

Well, I guess this was a temporary lack of judgment on my part as he wasn't quite ready to understand all of this clairaudient stuff. That would be forthcoming when he would have his own experience of hearing his angels. Yes, he heard them as if they were in the room with him! Thank goodness, he now understands the concept of clairaudience! It makes my life a whole lot easier!

For many folks, I think it takes something like what my husband experienced to convince them that hearing the divine world is indeed real. It is really unfortunate that in our society we consider this "voice hearing" to always be a sign of mental illness, no matter what is being said. I think that is why most people just keep their mouth shut about their experiences.

So, here's my last interesting experience from Hospital #3. There was one other occasion that Jesus came to visit me. He didn't speak to me but I definitely felt His presence. It was a little weird, but I actually felt as if I *was* Him. The only way that I know how to describe this is "being one with Jesus". I even remember peering into the mirror and feeling like I was seeing His reflection merged with mine.

I became very calm and wrapped a blanket around me, much like a robe. I then decided to take a short walk down the hallway of the hospital. I felt an amazing sense of freedom as I strolled my way down to a waiting area. I sat for a few moments on a bench and realized that the extreme muscle pain that I had endured over the last few years was almost completely gone. I also felt this wonderful sense of peace.

I know in my heart that I walked with Jesus that day. He was not by my side but within my very being. I could feel His love and healing energy deep within my very soul! On November 23rd, 2011, I asked if I could be discharged. I had spent a total of 11 days being hospitalized and I was ready to go home. The next day was Thanksgiving, and I didn't want to miss the celebration with my family. I had a lot to be thankful for.

Chapter Seven

Road to Recovery

My first night home after spending five days at Hospital #3 was a little unsettling. I don't remember dreaming but just felt like I was unconscious. I woke up at some point and realized that my sweet little dog, Bella, was licking me in the face. It was unusual for her as she had never done this before or since. She also tended to stay on my husband's side of the bed and not mine.

I really felt like she roused me from some sort of apnea episode or perhaps out of one of my unusual seizures. It's not too far out of the realm of possibilities. I was sent home with several medications that could have been a problem. Or, perhaps the wiring in my brain had not been completely repaired yet by my angel buddies.

What's really interesting here is that Bella normally didn't sleep with us. She had only started sleeping in the bed with me a month or so before when I was frightened about the "ghosts" that I believed were in the house. I knew that dogs were extremely sensitive to spiritual activity and felt at the time that she would alert me if there was a problem.

I realize now that it wasn't necessary for her to warn me about any spirits in the house, but have to wonder if the purpose wasn't more about my first night home. Perhaps my friendly ghosts frightened me just enough so that I would allow her to sleep with me. I know that God or my angels could have roused me, but they could have also set the stage for it to happen through what is considered an ordinary means.

Even though my first night home was a little disturbing, my first full day home was just the opposite. My house was buzzing with activity as the Thanksgiving meal was being prepared. What was really different this year was that I didn't have to do a darn thing! My husband and kiddos took care of organizing the whole dinner and I got to sit back and relax.

I almost laughed out loud when my oldest daughter, Amy, got frustrated and began to yell at everyone to get out of the kitchen! I had heard my mother-in-law use those same exact words almost every Thanksgiving since I married into her family! It was as if Barbara had stepped in to let us know that she was there and taking charge! That's when everyone would go scurrying out so she could finish preparing the meal.

Just like in the old days, everyone scampered out of my kitchen and things settled down. I'm not really sure why we had so many people there that year. The celebration at our house had been getting smaller since most of the kids were grown and had their own families to celebrate with. I'm not sure who was in charge of the guest list, but I was certainly glad to see everyone!

It was on this day that I noticed how easy it was for me to get up off of the couch. I remember touching my legs and not feeling any pain. I know that my energy level was better as I was walking around the house quite a bit more. I felt like something was different but I still didn't completely understand what had happened. I really enjoyed the day but a lot of it was rather fuzzy. I was feeling a little bit like a space cadet from one of the medications that I was taking.

After Thanksgiving, the house got quiet again and I realized that I was having more undesirable side effects. Not only was I a little confused and spacey, but I was having some visual disturbances. Well, that did it. I decided that it was time to make a change and I consulted with my angels. I asked them about each one of the prescriptions that I was taking and they guided me into the appropriate way to wean off of them. I systematically began the process of discontinuing everything as they said I didn't need them. Then I began to clean out my medicine cabinet.

Day after day, I carried pill containers to the bathroom and began to flush pills down the toilet. I contemplated throwing them in the trash but my angels said it was better to flush them. I knew that all of those chemicals could be a problem for the wastewater plant but they said it was the best solution. I can only imagine the chemical cocktail that went down my toilet.

It was so liberating that I decided to dispose of most of my supplements, too. I kept a few basic things but even began questioning the need for those. Don't we get enough of everything through our foods? On top of that, could there be toxic ingredients mixed in with the supplements? Well, the answers were "we should" and "there might be". I also disposed of that huge pill container that I had been chained to for several years.

It was an unusual but liberating feeling to get up in the morning and not swallow any pills. At some point, I even realized how much money we were saving! Even though we had insurance, the co-payments had been adding up and that didn't include the cost of my supplements. I calculated that we were now going to easily save several hundred dollars each month!

As my body began to adjust to withdrawing from the rest of the medications, several things began to happen. Some were pleasant and some were not so pleasant. It was nowhere near as traumatic as what happened in the hospital, but it was still an ordeal for me. But, there was a silver lining to all of the unpleasant stuff.

Several issues developed but my angels helped me to work through each and every one of them. It was a major learning experience for me and I was encouraged to document most of it. I know that at the time I didn't completely realize the scope of what was happening. I was just too busy working through each problem that arose.

Fortunately, the spells where I felt like I stopped breathing began to subside which made a huge difference for me. Those spells had reminded me of an incident several years prior where I had awakened with an asthma attack. There is nothing worse than feeling like you can't breathe. Or should I say, there is nothing worse than the feeling you get when you are not breathing.

At any rate, I was glad that my spells were going away. As I write this, I am wondering if I had been experiencing some form of nocturnal asthma or other problem. At some point, my angels had steered me into an article that discussed how patients with neuromuscular disorders were prone to "sleep disordered breathing". I had also found another article that was quite interesting. It addressed how neuromuscular patients may suffer from what is called "nocturnal respiratory failure" even though they have no problems during the daytime.

I think the point of finding those articles is to advise those who have a neuromuscular disorder to avoid taking sleeping medications. The muscle weakness that already exists can be exacerbated by the medication and can have life threatening complications. I guess that I was very fortunate to have my angels by my side during my illness and withdrawal!

Although the spells were going away, I was still having a few other sleep issues. I sometimes could only sleep fifteen minutes at a time as my bladder kept waking me up. No matter how early I stopped drinking fluids, my urine production just didn't slow down. It wasn't just a sensitive bladder; it was absolutely necessary for me to relieve myself. I know that my body could have been simply readjusting to not having medications tell it what to do. But, I have to wonder if there wasn't more to this. Maybe the interrupted sleep was necessary while my body finished healing. It might have been important that I not enter the later stages of sleep for a little while.

So, for several nights, I only slept fifteen minutes at a time. I began to pray for longer sleep periods and it did happen on occasion. I don't know why, but I logged how many times I got up. I guess it did make me feel better to know when I was making progress. My angels told me not to worry about the sleep issues as they would resolve on their own. I was a little concerned for awhile as I had been on a medication that had interfered with my Stage Four sleep. I wasn't sure how long it would take me to return to a normal sleep pattern, but I didn't worry about it.

I do know that lack of restful sleep is a big issue for many folks and I have since learned a few other things to help with the issue. One of the recommendations from my angels was to stop thinking about stuff that was not important. They encouraged me to just think about pleasant thoughts and I would drift off to sleep. If there was something that was important to remember, they instructed me to get up and make a note so I could deal with it the next day. Otherwise, they said that there should be nothing going on in my mind of major concern. Too many times, people mull over the day's events and start to stew and worry about issues that they have no control of. It is best to let go of everything in order to get a good night's rest.

It is also helpful to do something enjoyable prior to turning in for the night. The happy thoughts will set the stage for a pleasant night's sleep. I definitely remember sleeping very well on a night after having a good laugh with one of my daughters.

Angels can also help people sleep who are trying their best but are still unsuccessful. All they really need to do is to ask them for help. Their help will show up in a variety of ways. One way is to send you a visual image of something that interfered with your sleep. An example would be suddenly thinking about a clip from a horror movie that you just watched and realizing that it affected you. Another example would be by thinking that you are smelling coffee and realizing that you took in too much caffeine that day.

There are many other ways that angels will communicate the issues to you but it is too complicated to share in this book. Their purpose in this is to teach us how we can make the necessary changes and avoid the problems. Sometimes, though, we can still have an occasional bout of insomnia and they will assist with this as well.

When this happens, just ask them politely to help you fall asleep. I have done this many times and most of the time, I drift right off! I have affectionately nicknamed a few angels to make it easier to talk to them. The first one I named "Cammie". This was short for chamomile tea, which is an herbal tea that helps you sleep. Don't laugh, but occasionally "Cammie" did not show up so I asked for "Mellie" (a shortened version of melatonin, another sleep remedy). Then someone told me about Valerian Root tea. Yes, I named another angel, Valerie.

Every once in awhile, I would ask all three of them to help me get a good night's sleep. I usually would be asleep before I could even utter the name Valerie in my head. What's amazing is that I could actually hear certain tones inside my head that were let's say, hypnotic. I also could tell that my body would begin to relax. That's when I would remember to tell them thank you. They do like it when we appreciate their efforts!

My angels do want me to clarify something here. I'm not recommending that you take any of the above mentioned teas or supplements. I'm simply sharing how I came up with their names. It is best if we fall asleep in a natural manner. The repercussions of sleep medications, even natural ones, can be very dangerous and should be avoided, if at all possible.

Even though my sleep was improving, I had an incident that I found quite intriguing. It must have been significant, as my angels told me to write down what happened. I woke up with a severe headache that I thought was attributed to muscle spasms. Then, I sneezed twice and blew my nose. I heard three popping sounds that sounded like they were coming from my throat and my headache immediately got better. My nose, which had been stuffy, also cleared up and I could breathe much better.

Now, I don't know what happened but believe that there was some sort of significance to this. I haven't felt the same kind of popping in my throat since that happened. I don't recommend that anyone try this as it was probably a customized technique to assist in my recovery. It was not the first time that something like this happened and certainly would not be the last. When we ask for help, our angels will guide us right into all kinds healing.

In addition to helping with sleep related issues, my angels also helped me with my muscles. I had a noticeable increase in strength and flexibility but I also had severe muscle spasms. I am not sure if it was because they were waking up after years of decline or if it was a side effect of a medication that I had recently discontinued. I'm guessing a little bit of both.

I was encouraged to sit on the floor and stretch whenever possible. They also recommended that I get a massage and go see my chiropractor. I was having some neck issues and knew that she could take care of it. What is interesting is that although I was having lots of spasms, my chiropractor immediately noticed how much more flexible I was. And I really had not been doing much stretching at that point!

There were a few times that I did become a little frightened about the spasms. They were so severe in my neck that I feared they would interfere with my ability to breathe. The muscles kept contracting up and I couldn't figure out a way to get them to stay relaxed. Actually, the muscle contraction became so prominent that I originally thought I was developing a goiter. I visited my endocrinologist and he was the one that told me it was a contracted muscle. He magically applied the pressure for it to release and told me that it was probably a side effect from one of the medications that I just got off of. Interestingly, it was never quite as bad after that.

I was also still experiencing some fairly major anxiety issues. Evidently, I was experiencing what is known as "rebound phenomenon." One of the medications that I had been taking was a benzodiazepine that had been prescribed for insomnia. After the medication was stopped, I experienced sleep issues again plus the compounded problem of anxiety.

After my recent experiences in the hospital, though, I wasn't about to take anything for it. I decided that I would just deal with the anxiety and I had a great support system to help me get through it. My angel buddies were there for me and encouraged me to do several things. I really recommend that if you are having anxiety problems, that you give the following techniques a try!

I was encouraged to avoid watching anything on television that was violent or even too adventurous. Those shows are way too stimulating to a nervous system that is trying to heal. That meant that I also avoided watching the news entirely. I focused on shows that basically had no activity to them. I don't remember what they were but they were probably a little boring to me. I'm guessing that I was just listening to the sounds and background noise. This was actually what helped put me to sleep.

I have since learned that some cartoons are also very beneficial and therapeutic for a number of reasons. The storylines are usually non-threatening and most just provide simple entertainment. The colors are also pleasing to the eyes and this helps us to relax. There is a lot to be said about visual stimulation and how it can affect brain chemistry.

With that in mind, coloring with crayons can also help with anxiety. In addition to the colors being soothing to the eyes, the act of coloring soothes the soul. It sparks memories of an innocent time when life was not so complicated. Regressing back to this time for a little while can allow those frayed nerves to heal.

Another easy way that I was taught to deal with anxiety was to walk it off. The floor plan to our house is set up so that I could walk circles through the rooms without ever disturbing my husband. I don't even think that he was aware of how many times I lapped the house! The exercise must have somehow helped me process out the bad chemicals and helped me to relax. I'm sure it also stimulated the production of good chemicals in my body as well. And, as an extra perk, I was able to burn off a few calories at the same time! Those angels are really good at helping us multi-task!

Another way that they helped me in dealing with anxiety was to pay attention to the way I was breathing. They encouraged me to breathe slowly and to focus on the rise and fall of my abdomen. Sometimes we breathe too fast from the upper chest and this causes hyperventilation. This is a great technique to use when you feel a wave of anxiety or fear coming over you. It is very simple but amazingly successful. Many of the symptoms of anxiety are caused by shallow breathing and hyperventilation. This can create lightheadedness, shortness of breath, rapid heart rate and even chest pain.

Those breathing techniques should also be used in combination with what I consider the distraction method. It's important to not stay focused on unpleasant thoughts. Those thoughts only create fuel for the anxiety to continue. Redirecting those thoughts to something more pleasant is important for good mental health. If there is an issue that needs to be dealt with though, it's important to train ourselves to be able to handle it.

Initially, my anxiety about certain things was tremendous, so I just redirected my thoughts onto something else that was enjoyable. When the severity of the anxiety subsided, I could address the issues that were triggering it. Gentle and brief exposure was important as well as adjusting my perception.

I know this sounds complicated so I'll give you an example. Every time I looked at my medical records from my hospital stays, I became anxious. I could feel my heart speed up and I felt sick to my stomach. What I really wanted to do was to throw them away and never look back. But that is not what my angels instructed me to do.

They encouraged me to sift through them a little at a time and jot down a few notes. When I got overwhelmed, they told me to set it aside for another day. When I felt strong enough, they told me to repeat the process. I eventually made a timeline and extracted a wealth of information. It was a very long and tedious process but I managed to gather all of the information that I needed for this book. At some point I realized that the information that was in those records could benefit thousands of others. I couldn't just tell people that I was healed during my hospital stays. I needed to share the details.

I also didn't realize at the time that going through my medical records was vital to my emotional healing about the whole ordeal. I needed to see just what happened to me and change my perspective about it. In the beginning, I looked at those records and saw a painful reminder of the most traumatic experience I have ever endured. Now, I can look at them and see the absolutely amazing and phenomenal manner in how God performed my miracle. Sometimes, we just have to change our perspective about things.

I don't know exactly when it happened, but I began to get to know the different angels that were taking care of me and their roles in my life. I know that there were many involved in my healing and recovery although I haven't been told of an exact number. Of course, I keep asking questions about it as it still fascinates me. I have been told that I will get to know more about all of the angels after I finish this book and am really looking forward to it!

I remember while in the hospital hearing one in particular that had a very comforting voice. She was the one that always told me that I was going to be just fine. I believe that this was my guardian angel and she provided me a lot of comfort even after I got home from the hospital. Whenever I was feeling upset, I could hear her encouraging words and I usually shed a few tears. She always knew exactly what to say to me and in the most incredibly soothing voice that you can possibly imagine. I ended up hearing her quite a bit in the weeks following my hospitalization. You see, my angels had me on an extremely fast track for rehabilitation and I got frustrated a time or two. But, I always trusted them as they knew what was in my best interest!

That fast track didn't just include the physical rehabilitation but included a good workout on my brain as well. So, while I was dealing with sleep, muscle and anxiety issues, they began to stimulate my cognitive processes. One of the ways that they did this was to challenge me into these wonderfully thought provoking conversations. I remember that we briefly discussed politics, world events, religion, sexuality and many other topics. There were some days that I was exhausted from all of the conversations in my head.

I realized at some point that angels had the answers to everything. When I realized this I began to ask all kinds of questions. You may not believe this, but my first real question would probably surprise you. I asked them "Who shot Kennedy?" I know, in the whole scheme of things, it really doesn't matter. And that's exactly what they told me.

I asked all kinds of other questions but I didn't always get an answer. One day, I asked if they could help me with a computer issue that I was having. I guess they were still encouraging my brain to wake up as they steered me to the internet and gently replied "Look it up".

I realize now that there were many reasons for them to not give me direct answers. The research does stimulate the brain to work better but there is always more to it. The process of discovery can lead in to other significant findings that are also beneficial. I have since learned more about this "process" and don't question an indirect or misleading answer from them. They will always give us the information that is in our best interest. We have to remember that we are the children and we cannot see the bigger picture. It is important to trust God's messengers as they will assist us into living a life of happiness.

Focus and organization was also an issue with me so my angels instructed me to write everything down. It was odd for me to get overwhelmed as those areas were always my strong suit. But in light of everything, I guess it was pretty normal.

In addition to trying to keep up with the normal functions of running a household, the inspirational ideas started pouring in. I guess they didn't want me to sit back and relax too long. I ended up keeping several note pads laying around so that I could jot down whatever idea popped into my head. I didn't realize that they were also helping me document information for this book as well as for future ones!

During that first month of rehabilitation, I also learned a lot about emotional healing. My angels said that everyone can benefit from some kind of emotional healing. It is important to release all negative emotions for a complete healing. Many people hold on to too many of these negative emotions and it is doing them harm. This would include anger, resentment, shame, guilt, fear, worry, etc. It is also important to replace them with positive feelings such as peace, love, happiness, joy, harmony, etc. The negative feelings produce negative chemicals within the body and can cause illness; likewise, the positive feelings create positive chemicals within the body to help us be healthy.

During this release process, it is also best if we offer forgiveness to those who have wronged us. It is an important part of our own healing. By not forgiving, we are carrying the burden on our own back and it can interfere with our own well-being. The motto is "Forgive everyone for everything". This means that it is important to forgive ourselves as well. Too many times, we feel like we have made mistakes and we don't let ourselves off the hook.

They taught me about all of these lessons through what I would call a "living life review". I do believe that this was part of my training so that I could help heal other people. During this review, I was shown many different scenes from my life. For clarification, the review was not done in just one day, but over a period of time.

During some of these "scenes", I learned a lesson about guilt and shame. I "saw" a few instances where I had made poor choices during my life that I later regretted making. They reminded me of what led to the poor choices so I would learn from them.

I had actually already figured out most of the reasons that led to the mistakes, so the real focus for me on these memories was about forgiveness and releasing the negative emotions. We discussed how I had already made amends to anyone that was affected and I asked God to forgive me. They reassured me that He already had but that it was important for me to forgive myself. Most of these instances were not that major but I was still feeling a degree of shame and guilt about them. They instructed me to just let those emotions go as it was not beneficial for me to hold on to them.

As we moved from scene to scene, I was eventually shown scenes from my childhood that concerned my relationship with my mother. This memory also concerned the negative emotion of guilt. A part of me still felt like I had not been a good daughter to her. I didn't remember feeling very close and assumed that it was of my doing. My sister, Jamie, and I had been taught to not bother our mother about anything that would upset her. As a result, we were very guarded around her. I know that my father was trying to protect her as he felt that she was too emotionally weak to handle anything major.

What I needed to understand was that my behavior was very appropriate under those conditions and not to worry about it. With that in mind, they said that I should let go of whatever guilt I had for not feeling like I was a good daughter. They also told me that she is quite pleased with me and has been working with me for many years from the other side.

I also realized that I could apologize for whatever I thought I had done and she would still "hear" me. It is quite possible to ask for forgiveness from others even though they have moved on to heaven. Actually, it is encouraged so that those still living can move on in a healthier manner in their earthly life.

It also dawned on me that I could still have a relationship with my mother even though she is in heaven. My angels have already helped me to get to know her better while I was writing this book. I do believe that if it's important enough, it will continue in the future.

During my "living life review" I was also shown scenes from my childhood that were from happier times. It seems that I had forgotten most of them and had only remembered the unpleasant ones. I can't speak for everyone, but I feel like we tend to focus too much about all of the negative things that happened to us in our childhood.

Yes, those events affected us but they shouldn't define us. If dwelled upon, the unpleasant negative memory only serves to provide fuel for a negative future. We can't change the past. It's important to learn something from those experiences and move forward in a positive manner. It would be best if we focus on the positive things in our lives and encourage others to do so as well. This is what will be the catalyst for a peaceful future for all of humanity.

I have been told that anyone can access their own "living life review" if they so desire. It's a great way to do emotional healing work. I have a strong feeling that this is going to be an area that they are going to have me work on so that I can assist others in their very own healing!

Other scenes that I was shown during my training period involved what I would call embarrassing moments. What I learned out of this was that my angels knew everything about me. And by that I do mean EVERYTHING! They knew all of my deepest thoughts and had seen every action that I had ever taken. No matter what you do, there just isn't anything that you can hide from them or God. In their eyes, your life is truly transparent.

So, if you are cheating on your taxes, I don't think that it is "Big Brother" that you should be concerned about. It would be best if you live your life in the manner that our Maker would want you to live it. If you are having difficulty, always remember that you can ask for help.

As you can see, my first month of recovery was quite busy. I learned a lot of valuable lessons while getting some much needed rehabilitation. In addition to all of that, Christmas was just around the corner!

Chapter Eight

A Christmas to Remember

Just after Thanksgiving, I realized that I had lost valuable time to prepare for Christmas. I wasn't particularly worried about it as my angels kept me busy and on task. This year was very different than the previous few years as I could now perform all of the usual activities of a holiday preparation a whole lot easier. I kept thinking about how good I felt and my angels would always reply, "If you think you feel good now, just wait!"

There was only one time that I actually felt the old feeling of illness with full force. It was just a fleeting feeling but I was initially quite disturbed by it. They told me not to worry, that the sickness was not returning. I believe that they wanted me to remember how bad it was as it was important for my story. I didn't continue to worry about the incident as they had not let me down so far! There actually wasn't much time for me to stew over it anyway. I was too busy with all of the usual preparations of shopping, baking, decorating and wrapping! And this year, I enjoyed every bit of it!

I normally bake about six dozen chocolate chip cookies during the week of Christmas. What was different this year was the intense hip pain from standing in one position had completely disappeared! My stamina was also better and I could hold my hand mixer without difficulty. Yes, I still like to use a hand mixer when I bake. I have a really big one that my father gave me years ago, but I like to mix my cookies up in individual batches. My theory is that if I mess it up, I only ruin one batch. As my family knows, I'm very particular about those cookies!

During this same time, I think my angels gave me a slight reprieve in my mental rehabilitation. They actually helped me pick out Christmas gifts for everyone on my list! It was really quite interesting as to how it all worked. Like many people, I usually look at all the sale ads to get inspiration for just the right presents. This year the inspiration was noticeably ramped up and I ended up with several ideas for each person. What was really neat was that they somehow guided me to be at just the right place at just the right time so I could also get the best prices!

A Christmas to Remember

I felt so good that year that I actually enjoyed shopping for those gifts. It was such a liberating feeling to be able to move freely about without overwhelming fatigue and constant pain! Plus, there was no longer a need for me to ride in a motorized scooter to get around! I remember feeling rather giddy as I walked through the stores listening to Christmas music. I think I was even humming. Yes, I was walking and humming to the sounds of Christmas! It's still hard to believe that I did all of this right after getting out of the hospital!

And, as any really good shopper does, I took advantage of those sales and bought myself a few things, too. One of those items was a "guardian angel" necklace with the words "Watch over me" on the back. What is rather amusing is that I started not to buy it because it did not have the word "please" on it. Yes, I'm a real stickler for being polite. But, my angels told me to go ahead and buy it anyway.

That actually brings up another rather amusing etiquette dilemma that I faced while I was learning to talk with them. If I couldn't understand what they said, I didn't know whether to say "ma'am?" or "sir?" as I couldn't distinguish if the voice was female or male sounding. So, in the end, I just opted for a very polite "Yes?" Betcha never thought about that kind of dilemma!

Eventually, I could tell the difference between the voices and began learning more about their personalities. There was one time in particular that I could actually discern five separate voices talking at the same time. There were probably more, but I could only distinguish five. You may think that would be difficult to do, but it really wasn't. I just listened to them like I would listen to music.

Imagine listening to a symphony and focusing your ears on the violins playing. You will still hear the other instruments, but the violins will be your focus. You should be able to hear their melody as primary and the rest of the instrument melodies will be in the background. After that, you can switch your focus over to another instrument and do the same thing. For those of you that are musically inclined, this is probably a snap. For me, it was a little more difficult in the beginning. I must say, though, that listening to their "symphony of voices" was absolutely amazing!

When I really got better at hearing them, the messages became much clearer. There are absolutely no words to describe the emotion that I felt the first time that I heard them say "We love you". Three simple words. I remember bursting into tears as I realized the pure unconditional love that they were offering me! And I happily responded with an "I love you all, too!"

It's important to remember to tell those that we care about of our feelings of love. Although the words are important, it is also good to show our love through our actions and behavior. I always try to do this with those that I care about but sometimes I am not always successful.

There was one occasion that I was once encouraged to apologize to my husband after I had gotten a little unkind to him. My angels were not accusatory but somehow pointed out what I had sounded like. They are very good at letting us know about our mistakes in a manner that is easiest for us to accept. Generally, this is through our feelings about what happened and it is important to pay attention to them.

Even though I can hear them talking, I do try and pay attention to what I'm feeling so that I can merge the two messages. On that particular occasion, I felt a tad bit guilty about being unkind. I guess I could have been stubborn and not apologized, but then I would have let my angels down. Plus, it would not have been good for my relationship with my husband. So, I made amends!

I also know that there will be times in the future where I will make more mistakes and need to make more amends. The important part is realizing what those mistakes are and doing my best to rectify the situation. With the help of my angels, though, I am hoping that they will be at a bare minimum!

So, getting back to Christmas. In many ways, this particular Christmas was a lot like the one that I celebrated right after my coding incident. There is something about a brush with death that seems to strengthen your connection to God and the divine world. This year, I could also say that I had a more personal relationship with Jesus. I decided this year to invite Him to our family gathering and my angels told me that He would be there. They also reminded me that He had been to my home a few months earlier when Kim and I were trying to cross spirits over into heaven. That particular time, she and I both had felt His presence. It was really amazing!

I was so happy and I really wanted my entire family to feel the same spiritual "warm fuzzies" that I had been feeling. It is kind of like having a good recipe. You enjoy it so much that you want others to enjoy it as well. I knew that it was very possible that there could be some special sign so I tried to facilitate it. I bought some white unscented candles to place in the bathroom with the expectation that they would mysteriously emit a rose fragrance. I had once smelled roses without them being present and it immediately made me think about Jesus. I thought that if others could smell roses, they would think the same thing. Well, that is not necessarily true. I have since heard that other people think about His mother, Mary when they smell roses.

In reality, there is no correct or incorrect association. It is a personalized experience. Whoever you think about is who is present. I won't elaborate here but will tell you that the experience is a clairsentient experience and happens to a lot of people. It is one way that the divine world communicates with us. For example, if you smell your deceased grandmother's perfume and think about her, then she is probably present with you and letting you know that she is there. Or, the smell is triggering a train of thought that is important for you.

Anyway, I decided that there were too many children present to put lit candles where I couldn't keep an eye on them so I scratched the plan. I also contemplated trying to get everyone outdoors to see if there would be an angelic sign. I really believed that there was a good chance that my angels would manifest in some way for everyone to see them. I ended up scratching that plan as well for several reasons. I wasn't really sure that they were all ready for something unusual to happen plus it was cold outside. I also realized that they might think I was a little nuts.

I still kept my hopes up, but I actually forgot to keep an eye out for anything odd to happen. Well, that is what happens when you have about forty people in your home and everyone is having a good time! I think the only warm fuzzies that anyone got was when the mealtime prayer was said. It began with the children saying, "God is great; God is good; Let us thank Him for our food." It was promptly followed by "Good God, let's eat!" by a few hungry adults.

As my spiritual training progressed, I learned more about how the signs from the divine world really work. I learned that timing is important and it was simply not the right time for something supernatural to happen in my living room on Christmas Eve. I also learned that I don't have to orchestrate the event at all. If it is going to happen, it will happen without me getting involved. I also learned that we don't have to know when to pay attention. If it is important enough, our attention will be directed towards a special sign. That is just how it works. This happens all the time but many tend to believe that it is just a coincidence.

So, even though I didn't witness any special signs at Christmas that year, I know that Jesus and other heavenly beings were present with us. From what I have been told, there is no limitation in where His spirit can show up. I have also been told that He accepts all invitations to celebrate His birthday! I also believe that my mother-in-law was in attendance as this used to be her shindig. I simply can't imagine that she wouldn't still be celebrating with all of her family! I believe that there are quite a few other family members that would agree with me!

I know that on the following Christmas Eve my oldest daughter, Amy definitely felt her presence. While sitting on the couch, she had a very unusual experience. It seemed as if a baby dragonfly had made its way into the house and landed on her leg. By the time Amy got my attention, it had flown away. I thought that was kind of odd so I did some research to see if it is common to have baby dragonflies buzzing about in December in south Texas. I didn't find out much about their life cycle other than that baby dragonflies don't have wings. I think they live in the water until they grow wings and then they are considered to be adult.

So, I guess she saw a miniature version of an adult dragonfly or some other insect species. No matter what it was, it doesn't really matter. We both found it odd that an insect that is known to be spiritual in nature had made its way into the house during our Christmas Eve celebration. And it took the time to land on her lap and say hello.

I was originally very disappointed that I missed seeing it and chided myself a bit for not hearing her. As I pointed out earlier, though, I would have looked in her direction if I was supposed to see it. Evidently, this particular sign from above was meant for her and whoever else saw that dragonfly.

In addition to the dragonfly sighting, other unusual phenomenon began to happen during subsequent Christmas celebrations. I began feeling like there was a presence at various locations in my house and began taking pictures of those areas. One area included my stairwell, where I had also felt a spiritual presence during other times of the year. I was super excited when I saw that some of those pictures were filled with tiny orbs!

In addition to the stairwell, orbs showed up in several other pictures as well. My daughter, Kim, even captured some unusual light phenomena on her camera. I know that sometimes you can catch dust particles that catch the light just right, but I feel like most of these were not dust. A few of them looked too odd to just be dust. And besides that, my angel friends told me that they were not all dust!

Kim and I also captured more unusual phenomena while at another family Christmas celebration at a different location. We now have these odd light anomalies showing up at two different locations from two different cameras! I decided to review pictures from previous years to see if this had been happening all along but couldn't find much. It seems as if we are now beginning to see something very extraordinary happening! My only guess is that we have now begun to draw in a very strong spiritual presence. I am super excited to see what will happen during our future Christmas celebrations!

Even though we didn't witness any divine signs that first Christmas after my healing, there was something extraordinary that happened. I do believe that I captured angel voices on a recording that I did. I had written a script to hand out to my family on Christmas Eve to share my story. I wanted them to know what had happened to me without sounding like a religious zealot. I also decided to record it hoping that there were messages on there that they would be able to hear. Although it was a little difficult for me, I could definitely hear angels on the recording that were separate from my real time hearing.

I also decided it was a good time to come out of the "clairaudient closet". Yes, I openly stated that I could now hear angels talking to me. As usual, the timing was interesting. I made the recording on December 19,

2011 which is a significant date for our family. I'll let you read what I wrote and then I'll share with you some of the messages from the recorded version!

Seventeen Months from Chimayo

Today is December 19, 2011 and I want to take this opportunity to record a message for my family. Something extraordinary happened to me seventeen months ago. My best friend, LeAnn _____, took me to Chimayo, New Mexico, where there is a sacred chapel that people visit and pray for miracles.

This is where I prayed for a miracle for my health. On July 25th, 2011, my daughter, Kim and I returned from Indiana where we visited a special friend, Donna _____. I went there to continue my quest for healing of my mind, body and soul. Little did I know of the things that God had in store for me.

In November, 2011, I experienced a horrible withdrawal from two addictive prescription drugs, _____ and _____. I faithfully prayed during this unpleasant time as I knew that I could die. As you all have witnessed, I did not die, but am making a full recovery from **_all_** of my illnesses.

These include: **_metabolic myopathy, fibromyalgia, hypertension, hypothyroidism, acid reflux and insomnia._** This is not by chance or some bizarre resetting of my system from the withdrawal. This is **_absolutely, positively, undeniably_** . . . the result of a miracle.

I know this because God sent my angels to take care of me. I prayed and they communicated with me the entire time. They encouraged me to keep my faith and that everything was going to be all right. I know that someone very special to all of us, who is on the other side, was instrumental in this. I also know that God granted me this miracle when I visited Chimayo, New Mexico on July 25, 2010.

Through this experience I have learned that **_anyone_** can receive a miracle by following three simple steps:

1. Take care of your mind – have a healthy mental outlook, learn new things and be a good person.

2. Take care of your body – don't smoke or do illegal drugs, only take prescription drugs when absolutely necessary and limit alcohol intake to a socially acceptable amount.

3. Take care of your soul – pray for a miracle of your choosing.

It is important to remember that there is no limit to the number of miracles that a person can receive and circumstances don't need to be dire for one to pray for a miracle. We tend to believe that we are only allowed one miracle and that we have to save it. This is not true. It is also good to pray for other people but we need to remember that in order to help others, we have to take care of ourselves first.

It's been seventeen months since my visit to Chimayo. I want to give thanks and appreciation for the divine intervention that saved my life. Thank you, God, Jesus, my angel friends, my spirit guides and all the white light heavenly beings who made this miracle possible.

I want to give special thanks to my mother-in- law, Barbara Catching, who left this earth nine years ago today, to continue on her spiritual journey in heaven. I love you, Barbara.

12-19-11

I remember the day that I listened to the recording of that script as if it were yesterday. I had put those headphones on and excitedly listened for angel messages to share with my family. And there were many. I not only heard messages for my family but other ones that were intended just for me. There were layers upon layers of melodic voices on that recording. I didn't realize it at first but those beautiful voices were not just talking. They were singing and rejoicing!

When I realized what they were celebrating, I began to cry. Tears streamed down my face as I listened to them tell me over and over that I had been healed! I was overwhelmed with emotion as I heard their messages.

"Cathy Catching prayed for a miracle and she got it! God granted her a miracle!"

> "*God gave a miracle to Cathy Catching!*"
>
> "*Oh, Cathy, you prayed for a miracle at Chimayo, New Mexico and it was certainly granted!*"

It was at that very moment in time that it all finally hit me. This was real and I had been healed! I could not only say it but I could feel it with utmost certainty! When I stopped sobbing, I realized that they wanted me to hear it for myself. They knew that hearing those words would make a difference to me. And it certainly did.

I continued to listen to the recording and heard other messages as well. Immediately following my verbal appreciation to everyone involved, I could plainly hear their responses.

> "*God said you're welcome, Cathy!*"
>
> "*You're welcome!*"
>
> "*You're welcome, Cathy!*"

They also left other wonderful messages for me to share with others. As I listened, I felt such an amazing sense of joy!

Angel Talk

"Praise the Lord!"

"Jesus wants us to pray for a miracle!"

"Everyone has their own angels; listen to the voices and use your intuition; your intuition will guide you to us!"

I also heard several other special messages that were meant specifically for my family! I became even more excited as I realized who they were talking about!

"Barbara Catching absolutely helped Cathy get a miracle!"

"It's Christmas Eve and Barbara Catching is here for her family!"

"Barbara Catching was in heaven but she's in this world to help her family pray for a miracle!"

"Let Barbara help you!"

"Barbara Catching has prayed for a miracle for all of her family and all they have to do is pray for themselves!"

"This is Barbara Catching!"

When I heard that very last message, I realized that my beloved mother-in-law was really there and communicating with me! I finally got a message directly from her! I had always felt that she was somehow involved in my miracle and I now had confirmation! It made me think about how thin the veil is between heaven and earth.

"There is another world out there that most humans call heaven. It is like a base camp where you go back to when you complete your special tasks/missions there on earth. Some of you return to earth very quickly in a new physical body and others hang around in heaven to assist those that are still earthbound. Those are the loved ones that some of you 'feel' around you at various times. There are also many other duties and assignments that spirits have after they have left earth. It is a timeless cycle and is difficult for most humans to comprehend. With this knowledge, though, most can find comfort in knowing that they never really die, they just move on to another place."

As you might have guessed, I didn't completely write those last two paragraphs! My angels have the most amazing way of working right through me!

I know that I must have been somehow guided into writing and recording the script about my healing for many reasons. One of them was to help me "feel" my miracle in a more powerful manner. Another one was to immediately begin spreading the message about the power of prayer to my family. You see, when people know that something is good and it works, they tend to try it out for themselves. Evidently, there were a few that must have begun to pray more. Over the next few months some interesting things began to happen.

Chapter Nine

Family of Miracles

Not too long after Christmas I began a research project. I had decided that I wanted to learn everything I could about Jesus, miracles and anything else that was related. I collected a few books and did some digging on the internet. I also picked up a Bible.

The more I read, the more confused I got. Although there were some amazingly inspirational stories, this book was also describing an all-mighty being that was vengeful, angry and destructive. I realized very quickly that this was not the God that I knew or the one that I had been taught about. Those particular traits sounded more like human ones than those belonging to a supremely divine being.

I did a little more research and found a little more information. As many know, the Bible actually consists of several books. They were written many years apart by many different authors. Those authors were men who believed that they were in connection with the divine world. Now, I definitely believe that humans can receive divine information as this is what I do. I also believe that there is much in the Bible that was channeled directly from God or one of his messengers. But, there is too much contradiction to be able to take everything at face value. There is a good chance that somewhere along the way that there was interference by men to skew the messages in their favor.

It's important to remember that the early churches and government were heavily involved in the teachings and interpretations of the Bible. They could have been corrupt or they could have had good intentions but misguided in what they thought was best for all concerned.

I decided to read the Bible along with other religious and spiritual articles with a healthy dose of skepticism. While doing so, my angels would occasionally ask me to interpret what I read. Their ultimate question to me was, "What did I *feel* about what I just read?" Eventually, I learned that they were teaching me on how to trust my "gut feeling" about the information. As I explained in an earlier chapter, your "gut feeling" or your "instinct" is your direct connection to the divine world. It is how that world steers you in the right direction. I call it your "direct pipeline to God" and everyone can access it.

As I read through the religious and spiritual articles, I took the time to acknowledge what I felt about the information. The lesson for me was to trust that instinct and not believe everything that I read.

I realize now that this is probably the same conclusion that my father came to. He was not very fond of organized religion but chose instead to follow his own spiritual path. We didn't go to church on Sunday but were taught our weekly "sermons" from the comfort of our own home. We were given a weekly lesson of his choosing and were quizzed about it the following week. Even though I wasn't fond of the schooling at the time, it did provide the foundation of spirituality that I still carry with me today.

Through these lessons, my sister Jamie and I learned to respect other people without prejudice in an era that was recovering from racial turbulence. As man was learning how to walk on the moon, our dad taught us how to walk in someone else's shoes here on earth. While a bitter war raged throughout Vietnam, we learned about love and peace.

Simply stated, we learned how to be good people. We also learned to believe in a loving and forgiving God. One of my dad's favorite sayings was "My life is my gift from God; what I do with it is my gift to Him." This was one of his many sayings that he liked to share and was a special one between him and my daughter, Katie. I feel sure that he shared it with all of us but she is the one who seems to remember it the best.

In many ways I feel like my dad taught us to be just like Jesus, even though he didn't teach us about Him. I remember my dad acknowledging that Jesus was a good man, but he wasn't convinced that He was the son of God. I am speculating here but believe that his doubt had to do with the mixed messages that he got from the Bible. It also could have been through exposure to hypocrisy or a few overly religious zealots.

Sometimes there are those who are trying to spread God's message that get a little too carried away with their own personal philosophy. They try to convince others into their way of thinking which is not what God wants. He wants all of us to come up with our conclusion about who He is and obtain our own personal relationship with Him.

Another concept that was somehow missing from our spiritual training concerned miracles and faith healing. I know that my dad had some kind of exposure to the concept as his mother was of the Christian Science faith. They have a strong foundation in faith healing.

He once told me a really amazing story that his mother had shared with him.

That story was about a baby boy who suffered a broken collar bone during birth in the early 1920's. This little fellow was also underweight and extremely lethargic. The doctors couldn't do anything for him and told the parents that he would most likely not live through the night. The child's mother took him home from the hospital and contacted prayer warriors from her Christian Science church. As the story goes, they held a prayer vigil for the baby boy throughout the night. He not only survived, but lived to the ripe old age of 83 years old.

I really don't remember what my father actually believed about that story. He evidently wasn't sure that it was a miracle as this wasn't how he relayed it to me. It was just more of a factual accounting. What is rather surprising to me is his uncertainty in the matter. You see, he was the baby boy that received the healing.

Even though I didn't learn much about faith healing, what I did learn as a child was to pray. My sister and I were both taught our bedtime and mealtime prayers. It was such a natural part of who I was although I don't remember talking much about it. My angels helped me to remember how much this had been a part of my life.

They also encouraged me to share about how important it is to teach our children about the power in prayer.

I now realize that God had heard me praying about my health from the very beginning. I was doing everything that I needed to do to qualify for a miracle. I was a good person; I took care of myself; and I reached out and asked for help. He hadn't forgotten about me. It was simply a matter of His timing. And God always has perfect timing.

I know that some of you are wondering why I had to get so sick in the first place. I asked my angels the same question. In all reality, the unpleasantness of my illness was only a short part of my life. I now believe that there must have been a bigger reason for me to get so sick. Were there a few consequences of my actions that possibly delayed the healing? Perhaps. We need to understand that sometimes we do get in the way of our best interests. Is it possible that the illness and my healing were a part of my divine path? Absolutely. The entire experience is now a part of my story. And embedded within that story is the message about faith and the power of prayer that I can share with others.

As I shared in the previous chapter, I handed out a written script to relay the power of prayer to my family. Over the next several months, I began to watch as some amazing changes began to unfold around me. I am absolutely convinced that other miracles have occurred in our family and are continuing to happen.

The first miracle story that I want to share concerns my daughter, Kim. She is the daughter that I spoke about in Chapter Two that was experiencing the same symptoms that I had. I'll give you a little more background about her before I tell you about her miracle story. I have high hopes that one day she will share her experience in her own book.

After Kim was born, I decided that breastfeeding was the way to go. Her dad and I had taken special birthing classes to prepare for her arrival and our teacher really encouraged it. I had previously tried to nurse her older sister a few years earlier but gave up after about a week. I just felt too uncomfortable and restricted. I think that a lot of my lack of determination had to do with my young age and not understanding all of the wonderful benefits for the baby.

Anyway, I barely produced enough milk for Kim and never had any left to pump and freeze. Incidentally, after having my third child, Katie, I only produced a minimal amount of milk. And, as you may have guessed it, there was no milk by the time I had my fourth child, Michael. I think this lack of milk production is another link to the genetic illness as my mother was unable to nurse my sister and me as well.

Although I wanted to nurse Kim, I still felt like nursing was rather restrictive on me. I thought I would just supplement on occasion with a bottle of formula. But, no matter what I tried, she absolutely refused to take it. My mother-in-law and I were both of the theory that if she got hungry enough, she would drink from a bottle. We were both wrong. There was one occasion that Barbara babysat her and she cried until I got there to feed her. This really put some limits on what I could do but I just dealt with it. We kept trying and after nine and one half months, she finally decided to take a bottle.

I'm going on about this particular story for a couple of reasons. One is to stress the importance of mother's milk for children. There are many special ingredients in that milk that are of utmost importance for our children to get. It helps them get a wonderfully healthy start in their lives.

Another reason that I'm sharing this story is that I believe there is some divine significance here. I think that it was in Kim's best interest to have mother's milk. Even with that, she suffered with colic. I also think that the only way for her to get what she needed was for there to be no alternative. If she had started taking a bottle, I suspect that I would have stopped nursing her shortly thereafter.

In addition to colic, Kim tended to run unusually high fevers when she was a baby. They were the kind that would occasionally send us to the emergency room. There were other odd kinds of medical issues through the years with her but I won't go on about the rest of them.

As an adult, Kim is the only one out of my four children that was noticeably exhibiting symptoms of the same disorder that I had. She was having some difficulty folding laundry and intermittent trouble climbing stairs. I remember watching her and realizing that this was not normal for someone in their twenties. Those tasks should have been easier as she wasn't overweight and she ate a healthy diet.

I was very concerned about the possibility of her having the same illness as me. After I was healed, I really ramped up my prayers for her, my other children and my grandchildren. Every night, I talked with God about each one of them. I didn't want any of them to suffer. I shared with Him how much I loved them and what good people they all were. I asked Him to free all of them from this illness and to please show me if there was anything that I needed to do to help them. I even offered to take back the illness if he would spare them from it.

I continued my nightly prayers about this and tried to figure out if there was anything else that I needed to do. I wasn't sure that my children had completely understood my message from our Christmas Eve celebration. I guess that my concern was that if they didn't pray hard enough, that nothing would happen for them. I was also hesitant to keep talking to them about prayer. I felt like I might push them in the opposite direction. I thought about how I would have reacted and know that I would not have entirely listened. In all reality, I don't think that I would have completely believed my own story if I had heard it three years ago.

With all of that in mind, I decided to just take some actions that I hoped would spur them into prayer. I separated out the holy dirt that I brought back from Chimayo and gave each one of them a small vial. Since Kim was my biggest concern, I also decided to lend her my guardian angel pendant that I bought just prior to Christmas.

She called me a few days later with an interesting story. It seems that she went to sleep wearing the necklace. During the night, Kim began to toss and turn and had trouble breathing. From what I remember, she said she felt like she had stopped breathing. Anxiety issues were also a problem and she finally woke herself up. She realized that she had been experiencing the exact same symptoms that I had felt while in the hospital. She said that she just took the necklace off and she ended up sleeping better for the rest of the night. As I listened to her story, I realized that she wasn't very upset about it.

Initially, I thought this was odd as I would not have been very happy about having that experience. Then I realized that as an "empath" she probably believed that she was just "feeling" like I did and not really having problems. I'm assuming that she saw it as just temporary and that there was something to learn from it. I feel quite sure that she actually felt the same symptoms that I had while in the hospital. I originally felt a little upset about her suffering through the night but realized that there was a purpose for her to have that experience. I'm not sure of all of the reasons but I do have a couple of theories.

One is that it might be important for her to relay to others what it feels like to withdraw from certain medications. Her personal experience may help her down the road help someone from getting started on those drugs or help them get through their own withdrawal. There is something about going through it firsthand that allows us to help others with similar problems.

Another explanation for the experience is quite simple. I believe that there is a good possibility that God's divine hand touched and healed her on that night. I think that Kim believes this as well. It was not too long after that incident that she called me and told me that her muscles were stronger.

She was so calm and matter of fact that I really didn't know what she thought about it. I'm not sure if she was just being reserved or if she just had so much faith that it really wasn't much of a surprise. All I know is that there was never any question in her mind that she was being healed. I don't remember what I said to her but I wanted to shout out with excitement. I knew in my heart that this was another miracle! After we got off the phone and I calmed down, I began to weep with joy. My prayers and her prayers were being answered! She was not going to suffer any more!

I remember feeling as if an enormous burden had been lifted off of my shoulders as well. I could let go of feeling responsible for her illness. My angels had told me all along that she would be healed but I guess I still had some concern about it. I was still very new to all of this miracle stuff and I wasn't quite sure what it took to be healed. I have since let go of all of those worries and to just trust God to take care of all of my children and grandchildren. I can't control what any of them do. They are all in charge of their own lives and can create their own future. What I do have control over is my ability to pray for them and set a good example.

I got another phone call from Kim during the last part of January, 2012. She told me another very interesting story. Yes, it gets better. Sometime during the month, she realized that she had missed her normal dose of thyroid medication. She was a lot like I was in that she became very symptomatic after missing a dose. It's a little unusual to become very lethargic after missing just one dose, but this is what happened to both of us. If we missed two doses, we could barely get out of bed. I always believed that it had to do with the unusual metabolic disorder that we had.

Anyway, she realized that she had missed it and went back to her regular dose. Not too long after that, she remembered that she had missed it again for the second time. Again, she started taking it and didn't think much about it. Then it happened for the third time. That was when she realized that she was feeling just fine without it! I was ecstatic when she told me! This was the exact confirmation that I needed! To me, this was tangible enough proof that she had been healed!

I knew that God and His messengers had helped her accidentally miss that medication. That was their way of helping her to realize that she was well!

And the miracle stories in that household don't end here. She later told me that my four year old grandson's eczema had just disappeared! Gone, just like that! The skin disorder that had afflicted him since he was a baby was now gone!

Within a short time after that, he and his sister were both healed from a sensitivity to orange juice! They both had always experienced severe intestinal repercussions when they drank it so Kim didn't allow them to have it. She discovered that healing after a babysitter had inadvertently allowed them to drink it one evening. There were no repercussions that night or anytime thereafter! They could now both tolerate drinking a juice that had caused major problems for them their entire lives!

I think it's also important to note here that the miracle stories are not just limited to my blood relatives. I have been told that there are wonderful things going on for her other family members. Kim has a husband and a step-daughter that are receiving blessings as well! I just haven't heard about them just yet!

There have also been animal healings around us! One of Kim's beloved dogs, Hurley, developed epilepsy and almost died from it. She was put on a medication that was supposed to be taken for the rest of her life. It is not surprising to me that the dog no longer needs that medication and is seizure free! I firmly believe that Kim and her family healed their pet through prayer!

And speaking of animal miracles, I believe that my husband Mike actually healed our little Bella. She had developed a small tumor on her hindquarter that the vet had said to not worry about. He and I were still a little concerned about it as we had once lost a dog to cancer. He said that he prayed for it to go away and you guessed it. The little tumor just disappeared. I actually took her back to the vet and had them confirm it! I didn't hesitate to tell them what happened!

There were also some other unusual things going on with my daughter, Kim. My angels had told me that eventually she would be able to hear her angels, too. I know it has happened on at least one occasion. One night when she was singing karaoke, I noticed that she kept looking at the audience. I knew what was going on but I asked her what happened. She said that she distinctly heard a male voice singing with her. She was so sure that she kept looking around to see who it was. She and her husband own a DJ and karaoke business so she was very familiar with the background vocals in that song. According to Kim, there is no male background vocal in that version. She and I got a good laugh about it as we both knew that she had just had her first experience of what an angel can sound like!

Like I mentioned in Chapter Six, my husband even had his own experience with hearing angels. He also heard them in a male sounding voice and through music. I won't elaborate about it here but he has actually heard them twice, both times through the radio. I no longer have to convince him that they are very real and will talk to us when we are ready!

There were many other wonderful things that I began to notice about my immediate family in those first few months. That very first Christmas Eve when I handed out my script, they all appeared to be happier. I know that they could have just been happy that I was doing better but I don't think that was entirely it. I had the vague feeling that there was something more going on.

My son, Michael, was so happy that Christmas Eve that he openly declared his affections for his girlfriend. As far as I know, he had been fairly quiet about expressing his feelings so I was very surprised to hear him tell her that he loved her in front of everyone. I know that I could have just been paying more attention, but I don't think that was it. Two years later, he actually surprised her with a proposal of marriage during our Christmas Eve festivities. It was very exciting for all of us to be able to witness and be a part of this special event. And, by the way, she accepted and is now a member of our family!

In late January of 2012, my oldest daughter, Amy sent me the following beautiful message in an e-mail. I must confess that I still tear up when I read this!

> I tried calling you this morning to tell you "thank you". You have helped me find my faith. I wake up every day with a smile on my face feeling great no matter what. I feel better than I have in a very long time. Thank you for passing your miracle along to me.
>
> ::Amy::

It is a wonderful feeling to know that my experience helped her to find her happiness and her faith. I believe that it is her faith that will open doors for her in the future. I have been told by a good authority that there will be more miracles in store for her as well!

I actually believe that there have been other healings within her family. Her oldest daughter had been diagnosed with a genetic bleeding disorder a few years back. The last time I heard anything about it, she wasn't considered to have it anymore. The test results are now considered to be inconclusive and they have dropped the diagnosis! I didn't get all of the details but I really don't need them. My angels told me that she was also being healed. On my Chimayo recording I also heard them say that one of her other grandmothers had contributed to her miracle through prayer. How cool is that!

Amy's other daughter had an unusual experience as well. She suffered from a metal allergy so severe that she would break out with lesions on her belly whenever she wore a belt. One morning, she woke up and noticed that it was gone! Amy called me to tell me about it and for some reason I told her that it might come back. I wasn't completely sure what the reason was, but I knew that it would return. I have learned though, that there is a good reason for these things to happen and to trust that all is as it should be. I'm not sure of how much time has passed since then but I know now that my granddaughter evidently doesn't have the same sensitivity to metal. She no longer breaks out when she wears inexpensive jewelry! Coincidence? I don't think so. Miracle in progress? Absolutely.

I don't know what all has transpired with Amy's little boy, but I feel quite sure that something has changed or will change for him as well. I didn't notice anything right away as he was a healthy child. He seemed to come out of his shell a bit but I wasn't sure that it wasn't just a part of what happens at his age. At any rate, I have been told that he will have a wonderful future as well!

I continue to pray about all of my children and also talk to my angels about their future. One night while I was drifting off to sleep, I heard a very clear and soothing voice talk to me about my other daughter, Katie. The voice told me that "All of Katie's dreams are about to come true." I immediately woke up and felt this amazing sense of peace. I don't know all of the details, but I feel like she is receiving her own miracles, too!

In addition to my children, I feel like my sister is also receiving some sort of healing. I have to mention here that Jamie is probably the kindest person that I have ever known. There are times that I think that she may be an angel in disguise here on earth to teach us something. There seems to be a big difference in her happiness since my healing and I really look forward to seeing what is in store for her future! I already believe that she has been allowed to hear her angels just like me. There is no doubt in my mind that God is going to allow her to fulfill a lifelong dream of helping other people by delivering important messages from the angels. She has even delivered a few interesting messages to me!

Now, perhaps you are not quite convinced that there is something very unusual going on here. You may just think that all of the unusual healings are just coincidental. Well, keep on reading. I think that even the most staunch skeptics are going to be swayed.

I shared briefly in Chapter Two about a cousin of mine that was having unusual health issues. To refresh your memory, I had called her when I was sick to see what she knew about the family's health. I had been hoping to get information that would help me to get better. After my healing, I called her again to share what had happened to me. I wanted to encourage her to not give up on her own healing. As it turned out, I didn't have to inspire her at all. Seems like she somehow "stumbled" into a treatment and was feeling better. So much better that she believed that she was being healed. And she gave God full credit!

At some point, I realized that the miracles that were happening around me were not just in my bloodline. One of my brother-in-law's had been experiencing lung issues that I believed to be related to his line of work. He had some testing done and there were some abnormalities. I don't know what his exact diagnosis was but it is not really relevant. The last time we talked about it, he told me that he was much better. From what my angels have told me, his mother has been very involved in making sure that all of her family here on earth are being healed!

On that note, I'll mention what happened to my father-in-law. He had been diagnosed with a serious lung disorder that was environmental in origin. He seemed to be having some deterioration even though he stayed physically active. We all noticed that he was having coughing spells and I was concerned. My angels told me not to worry about him and guided me into sharing the benefit of natural medicine to him. I told him about the benefits of green tea and some other herbal teas and made a few suggestions. He was already a big believer in natural remedies so this was really not a new concept for him.

The next time I saw him, I noticed a huge change. He wasn't short of breath and the coughing spells were almost gone. He had chosen green tea and lemon as his treatment and it was working! I do believe that he was guided into the teas that would be best to help his particular condition. I also think there is something very divine in nature happening for him, too!

There was also another unusual finding on my husband's side of the family. One of my other brother-in-laws and his two children had been diagnosed with a genetic disorder that affected the growth of their bones.

One of those children has a daughter who had unusual stature and physical traits when she was little. I can't speak for everyone, but I think that most of us believed that she also had the disorder. There wasn't a genetic test done on her when she was little as I guess it didn't seem necessary at the time. Her doctors just treated her for the problems that she was having.

Now that she is a little older, they decided to do the test on her. As it turns out, she does not have the genetic disorder that her father, aunt and grandfather have! Now folks, explain that one to me. I feel quite sure that her DNA, just like mine, was repaired and that future generations will not have to be concerned with it anymore. As a matter of fact, I believe that the rest of her family are getting their own miracles as well!

As you can probably guess, I get a little excited when I talk to family members. I am just waiting to hear about something "unusual" happening to somebody. I know that there will be more to come and I'm really looking forward to documenting them!

In addition to the miracles going on around me, I am still experiencing more healings myself! Two of them involve my treadmill which is how I mainly get my exercise. Before I share these stories, though, I'd like to tell you what happened right after my healing. Not too long after my hospital stay, I began to walk on the treadmill. Actually, I wasn't home long before I started to run on the treadmill. My intention was to condition myself and go back and play soccer again! It was such a glorious feeling to have my life and my legs back that I just took off in an all out sprint. It was an amazing experience!

Well, it was amazing until I woke up the next morning. My knees hurt so badly that I could hardly walk. It seems that I had a lot of faith that I was healed! I simply discounted the reality that my body needed to rehabilitate from several years of inactivity! I know that my angels could have warned me to go slowly but they did not. I'm not sure if the injury was to keep me slowed down so some other stuff could heal or they wanted me to share this as a testament of my faith. By now, though, I have learned to trust that these kinds of things happen for a reason and are always in my best interest. Either that, or they are just not all that important in the whole scheme of things.

So, I slowed things down a bit and went back to walking on the treadmill. I also like to meditate at the same time so I shut my eyes and hold on to the arms. On one particular day, I was somehow guided to look down at my right elbow. I had been having a lot of problems with it and assumed it was from my illness and years of playing tennis. This was the same injured elbow that my angels had helped me to protect while in the hospital.

This is when I realized that I had experienced another healing. I immediately noticed that there was a developed muscle where there had previously been an indentation. I was then guided to look at the right arm of the treadmill while I was walking. The arm jiggled ever so slightly as there must have been a loose screw. I was then redirected to look back at my forearm. I watched in amazement as I made these tiny little muscle movements to compensate for that loose screw! I also suddenly realized that there was no longer any pain in that elbow!

I know that it may be a little hard to believe, but my angels led me right into rehabilitating my injured elbow without me even knowing it! It is beyond my comprehension as to how they orchestrated that healing! I know that this is what happened, though, because I have had other unusual incidents since then! Plus, they told me so!

On another occasion, they helped me with an injury to my right foot. I hurt it just after I returned to play soccer. Yes, I did get to go back and play! I had only participated a few minutes when I took a simple misstep.

I heard a popping noise and felt pain on the top of the foot. I had broken my right ankle several years earlier and wondered if the foot was a little weak. I was a little miffed again that my angels allowed me to hurt myself but wasn't too upset about it. There is always more to it than what meets the eye! Evidently, I had not done enough conditioning or the incident served another purpose.

After the injury, I tried for several months to rehabilitate my foot. I knew all of the appropriate exercises and stretches because of the broken ankle. I didn't feel like I was making much progress and I kept getting set back every time I tried to ramp up my walking efforts.

On one particular occasion, my angels guided me into an unusual stretch before walking. I took an unusual step backwards on the injured foot and put all of my weight on it. I bent my knee as if stretching my calf muscle and began lifting my heel up and down. I could feel the gentle stretching on the top of the foot and think there may have even been a few little popping sounds. I realized that this was not a stretch that I came up with but one that they guided my physical body into doing. I now continue that same stretch and no longer have any problems with that foot!

I realize now that if we ask for help and guidance, even if it is something minor, we will receive it! Sometimes it is not what we are expecting, but to just trust that it is in our best interest. It is also important to relax and pay attention to the signs and signals that the angels are delivering. Too often, people stay so busy and distracted that they miss them.

I actually had another incident that I was not very happy about but I learned a lot through the experience. I was moving too quickly trying to retrieve something from the landing of the stairwell and fell. I was trying to walk backwards down the steps and missed the last one. I actually hit the corner of the wall hard enough that it knocked the wind out of me.

When I realized what happened, I asked my angels if I was okay and they said yes. I was confused as to why it happened because I knew that they could have guided me to avoid the fall. I didn't give it too much more thought at the time and just redirected my focus on making sure that I was okay.

My back immediately began to spasm so I knew that I had hurt it pretty good. I tried to keep it stretched out by staying hunched over and crawled over to the couch. That is where I decided to make sure that all of my body parts were working properly. I stayed very calm and began to slowly move my feet, ankles, knees, hands, arms, etc., making sure that everything was okay.

When I had ascertained that there were no problems with my extremities, I began to slowly sit up. That's when I started to see spots although I didn't feel faint. I was puzzled so I hunched back over again and they went away. I waited a few minutes and tried to slowly sit up again. The same thing happened for the second time and I decided that this was not normal.

I called my husband and told him that I thought I needed to go to the hospital. As you can imagine, I did not really want to go. The very thought of it gave me extreme anxiety. The hospital had my medical records and I still had some fear from my last stay there. My angels told me to go so I pushed aside all of my fears and went to get evaluated. Since I was afraid to move, we decided to call an ambulance. I wasn't sure if something was compressed or restricted but I wasn't going to take any chances. I would sit up only after I was in the emergency room where they could treat me if something happened.

A few hours later, I could sit up without any problems so they let me go home. I have no idea why this all happened but I was never really worried about it. I did learn a few things out of the experience, though. One was not to be in a hurry about doing anything. I was definitely trying to move too fast that day and that is why I fell. I also continued to learn about releasing all of my fears. As you can imagine, it took a lot for me to return to that hospital.

I also learned how incredibly powerful green tea and common cooking herbs are for inflammation and muscle pain. I was already drinking a glass of green tea every day but decided to drink it every 4-6 hours after the fall to treat my symptoms. I also added the herbs to my diet that are known to be the best in treating inflammation. I drank the green tea plus added the herbs to my food in place of taking any muscle relaxers, pain pills or anti-inflammatories. I also began to gently stretch from the very beginning so that my muscles didn't draw up.

I noticed that the first day was the most problematic and I began to improve from that point forward. I thought that this was a little unusual as I always thought that the second or third day is usually the worst for a muscle injury. I'm assuming that I was doing better than average because I began the appropriate treatment right away.

I realized how good this treatment was after having a little setback. One afternoon I began experiencing more pain with my back and I was puzzled. As I reflected about my gentle stretching routine and green tea therapy, I realized that I had inadvertently skipped a dose! That was a real eye opener for me! I had no idea that this stuff was that powerful! I thought about how many people are poisoning their bodies with pain pills, anti-inflammatories, muscle relaxers, etc. when the treatment is quite simple. Stretching and natural anti-inflammatory foods would probably work for most cases! Plus, there are no awful side effects or long term repercussions!

So, even with a few little mishaps, my enthusiasm for life gets stronger every day. It is such an awesome feeling to know that we are not alone and that there is help available to all of us. I continue to watch my family and listen for more unusual stories so that I can continue documenting the family's miracles.

As I reflected back on all of the healings, I also thought about my trip to Chimayo, New Mexico. I began to feel a strong desire to return there and give my thanks to God for all that He has done for me as well as my family. In addition to giving my thanks, the trip would also serve as a nice full circle closure for this particular chapter in my life!

Chapter Ten

Return to Chimayo

A few short months after my healing, I went on a cleaning spree. It was a little early for an annual spring cleaning but that didn't matter. I was ready to get rid of a few things that I did not need or want. Among those items that I was ready to discard were my handicapped plates, wheelchair, walker, and cane. They had been useful for me while I was disabled but were no longer a necessary part of my life.

When my daughter-in-law told me that she wanted the wheelchair for her little brother, I got excited. He was having surgery and I was glad to be able to help out. I said a quick prayer for him and got the feeling that he was going to receive a blessing.

I decided to just give away the walker while having a garage sale. I taped a note to the seat that read "Owner of this walker received a miracle of healing." Just like my dad, I don't like to miss an opportunity to share an inspirational message! I felt like it was also blessed and wanted to make sure the future owner knew this!

I also thought it was a good time to change out my license plates. I was no longer disabled and didn't need to receive special parking benefits. My legs worked just fine and I didn't mind walking. It is good exercise and I certainly needed it! I was told that it was okay to simply discard them so that is exactly what I did. Yep, I tossed them in the trash! It was another wonderfully liberating experience!

As I thought about my return trip to Chimayo, I realized that it would be very appropriate for me to take my cane out there. I remember how inspired I got when I saw all of the crutches, canes and other items left there at the chapel. I think it sometimes takes something very tangible for people to be convinced that miracles really do happen. It just seems to make it more real. The items at Chimayo seem to serve as a visual testimony for others and I wanted to be a part of that! With that in mind, I saved the cane to take on my return trip.

Before I get too far into this, I want to share a few other interesting facts about my original trip to Chimayo. I didn't think much about it at the time, but there was a full moon while I was out there. I discovered this little item of interest after reviewing the pictures that I took. Another intriguing fact is about the timing of that first trip. During my book research, I realized that I visited the chapel on the anniversary of my father's death. I don't know what the significance is of these two pieces of information, but I do find it quite fascinating!

I was so excited about returning to Chimayo that I invited my entire family to go. I was hoping that we could make it a big family celebration but I knew that it would be difficult to coordinate everyone's schedules. As it turned out my husband, Mike and only one of our four kiddos could make it. It was our number three child, Katie, who lived about five hours from us. We don't get to see her as often as we'd like so it worked out wonderfully that she could go.

This trip reminded me of the ones that our family used to go on when she was little but with one major difference. This time, Katie got to be an only child! Perhaps there was a little divine intervention going on so that we could spend some really good one on one quality time with her!

We visited several places while in New Mexico and had a blast everywhere we went. Although we spent most of the time in the Santa Fe area, we also got to enjoy the scenery down the Turquoise Trail. I have to say that things look a whole lot different than what we see along the Texas Gulf Coast! We also retraced the steps from my previous trip and visited the Loretto Chapel and did some shopping in Santa Fe. Neither one of them had been there so it was a nice experience for all of us. We also got to visit a local winery which was on my hubby's list of things to do!

The highlight of the trip, of course, was our visit to Chimayo. In addition to taking my cane there, I wanted to visit with the chapel's priest. I had been in contact with him about trying to authenticate my miracle and wanted to chat about it. I also wanted to get more holy dirt to share with others.

Some of you may be wondering what is so special about that dirt. As far as I know, the dirt itself doesn't have any special curative properties. It is just ordinary dirt that has been blessed. But, it is something tangible that sparks people into praying and believing in miracles. It is the power in that faith that creates the miracle and that is why I believe the dirt is important.

During the drive north to Chimayo, my heart began to speed up in anticipation. I was very excited about returning to this special place that had been so important in my life. After we parked, I think I pretty much jumped out of the car wanting to hurry in to the chapel. I actually had to slow myself down a bit so that Mike and Katie could take a quick look around. In all reality, I didn't give them much time!

There were not very many people milling around so we easily maneuvered through the grounds. I had planned the trip to avoid the holy times as there are many who travel to Chimayo during those dates. If you are planning your own trip, be sure and check out their schedule to meet your own needs. From what I have seen, it is a beautiful and spiritual place no matter what time of the year that you are there!

As we got closer to the chapel, I thought about how easily I could walk the same path where I had hobbled along just two years earlier. In all reality, I could not only walk it easily, but could walk it quickly! I think I rushed everyone a bit as I still felt this sense of urgency to get inside. After zipping through the courtyard area, I stopped at the front door to make sure that we were all together.

As we slowly crossed the threshold, my eyes again had to adjust to the darkness inside the chapel. Immediately after that, something strange happened that genuinely surprised me. An intense emotion completely overwhelmed me and I began to cry. I tried to hold back my sobbing so I wouldn't completely lose it.

What I really felt like doing, though, was to fall to my knees right then and there and weep. Not because I was sad, but because I was happy! The best way to describe it is an overwhelming feeling of gratitude. I have to say that I wasn't at all prepared for that kind of intense and powerful emotional release.

After I regained my composure, I walked through the chapel and made my way to the side room. My intention was to just prop my cane against the wall but I saw a woman sitting in a wheelchair with her family. I assumed that she was there for a miracle to get out of that chair so I thought it would be appropriate to give her my cane. After explaining to her about my healing, she accepted my gift. My prayers were that she would be able to use it and be able to discard the chair. I thought that my story would somehow boost her faith about her own healing just a smidge.

After that, I wanted to get more holy dirt so it could be shared with others back home. I proceeded into that tiny room with a new feeling of confidence. This time, there was no need for help as I could easily squat down and get it all by myself! I left a small monetary donation in one of their boxes and felt like this part of my mission was accomplished.

I joined Mike and Katie and we all went back into the chapel. Since it wasn't crowded, we sat in the very same pew where I had prayed just about two years earlier. I reflected about everything that had happened to me and quietly gave my thanks to God and all of His heavenly helpers. In some ways, it was just a formality. I had been giving all of them my thanks every day since my healing.

Initially, I thought that my simple thank you was inadequate. What I really wanted to do was to give something back. It occurred to me later, though, that God is allowing me to do this through sharing my story. I can spread His message of love and hope by simply relaying what happened to me! On top of that, I can continue to keep giving back through the divine gifts that have been given to me! My abilities to directly communicate with the divine world are now allowing me to help people heal and live happier lives. What is really wonderful is that it also fulfills one of my lifelong dreams!

I didn't comprehend all of this while I sat there that day. I just sat there absorbing the atmosphere and enjoying the spiritual experience with my family. As I looked at each of their faces, I realized what a profound effect this place was having on them.

The man that I have loved deeply for thirty-four years was crying. Tears were trickling down his cheeks as I watched him look around the chapel. There have only been a few times in our marriage that I have actually seen him cry and it made me wonder. I wasn't wondering what he was thinking. I knew that he was emotional because of the spiritual presence of this place. What I was wondering was why haven't I seen him cry much? Was he discouraged as a child? Did it embarrass him?

I realized that these are real problems in our society. I think that too many times, we discourage boys from shedding tears. And, for what reason? Crying is a part of that built in release mechanism that God has provided for us. If more men would release their emotions through tears, perhaps we wouldn't have so much violence or as many heart attacks. I think that it is time that we stop viewing this as a sign of weakness.

I pondered over that a moment and then looked at Katie. I studied her face and reflected about the beautiful child that she was and still is. Not just externally, but on the inside. There were tears running down her cheeks, too, as she sat there and said a few prayers. She had asked her father and I to pray for a friend of hers whose father was very ill. We all did so and I thought about how kind she was. Her intention was to help someone else get through a rough time.

As I have since learned, though, it is very important to also pray for ourselves. It is not selfish to ask God for what we believe we need. It's really all about balance. With that in mind, I sat there and said a few more prayers for myself.

One of those prayers was for my eyesight to be healed. Not too long after my healing, I had gone outside to enjoy the beauty of the outdoors. The world somehow looked different to me. This was God's world and I realized how magnificent it really was! I looked around with a whole new perspective. The only problem was that it was very blurry.

I know that I could have put my glasses on, but it is just not the same as a wonderfully unobstructed view of the world. As I looked around, I had a sudden realization that God could heal my vision just like He had healed my body! I also realized that this would be an easier miracle to authenticate than my other one! I know that it is not necessary to prove anything but I somehow thought that it might help the little chapel in Chimayo. If they could somehow benefit, then perhaps more people could benefit.

At that time, I started to quickly pray for my eyes to be healed. Then, I hesitated. I thought that it might be too much to ask for and it might take away from someone else. My angels then told me to go ahead and pray for what I wanted and that no one else would be adversely affected. There is an abundance of miracles available and He loves handing them out. The saying is "Pray for what you want and God will give you what you need". We are not always guaranteed that we will get it, but to keep on praying.

So, I sat in that pew in Chimayo, New Mexico, continuing to pray that God would heal my eyesight. I really believed at the time that it just might be healed right then and there that very day. I also felt that I was actually going to know who was healing me. I have had several different visions of hands touching me on my forehead. One of those included Jesus, and as many of us know, He was very good at healing eyes!

After finishing up my prayers, I sat and waited for something to happen. I realized at some point that the healing was not going to happen right then. But, I was not discouraged as timing is always a factor! I know that if it is important enough, it will happen. I also know that it may not ever happen and I will understand.

With that in mind, I think that some people believe that God has let them down when their prayers aren't answered. What those folks need to remember though, is that He knows what the bigger picture is. It's important to just trust Him and be patient. I might also add that there are many occasions where people don't recognize that their prayers have been answered. They receive something that they were not asking for and don't always recognize the significance of it. It is important to always be thankful for what we are given and not focus on what we are not given. Positivity is what our world needs.

I had also been asking my angels to make an appearance at the chapel so I was looking for them as well. I was so hoping that my family and I would be able to see them! I also wanted to personally thank them for everything that they have done for me. After awhile, I realized that they were not going to manifest in front of me there at the chapel and I began to get a little antsy. I had wanted to talk with the priest and suddenly felt the need to get up. I asked my angels if it was okay to leave and they told me yes.

We all walked back towards the entrance where there was a small office area adjacent to the foyer. I stopped to speak with a woman who was working there and inquired about the priest. As it turned out, I had forgotten to make a firm appointment with him and he was unavailable. It's a little unusual for me to not have made a good plan and I was a little annoyed with myself.

While standing near the doorway, I noticed that there was some activity going on outside. It seems that there was a two man news crew just outside the front door preparing to film. That is when Katie looked at me and said, "Mom, this is meant to be. I think you are supposed to talk with them." Well, I completely agreed with her on that one! I chuckled to myself when I realized that this was probably the reason that my angels delayed me inside the chapel. Like I have said many times before, timing is always important!

I spoke with the news crew and learned that they worked for an El Paso, Texas news station. They were filming one of several segments about interesting places located along the Rio Grande River. Chimayo, New Mexico just happened to be one of their stops. They quickly made the decision to interview me after learning that I had been healed out of that chapel. I was a little nervous as there wasn't any time to prepare but I didn't mess up too badly.

The segment aired a few months later and I was thrilled! I know that it was only a few seconds of air time but I have to wonder what the purpose was. Could my story have helped one person? Was it a viewer or perhaps the news crew? We never really know how these things work but there must have been some significance. I do know that I got my first taste of publicity about my healing and my story added a little something to their news segment!

What's interesting is that I had been trying to get my story in the public eye from the very beginning. It wasn't about my desire for publicity but about having a positive influence on other people's lives. In order to spread a message you have to have a means to do so! I had not gotten an interview even though I contacted my local newspaper and one of my local news stations. I was getting a little frustrated but I remembered about having trust in the timing.

I decided at some point, though, that I would just get my message out there myself. I set up a page on a social networking site and posted my story. I visited my doctors and told them what happened so that they could inspire their patients. I made a list of all my friends and sent out e-mails and made phone calls. I began writing this book and made plans to write several more. It has been quite a lengthy task but I had a motive.

You see, my angels have told me how important it is for us to share the message. It inspires others into believing in something bigger than themselves. It boosts up faith and that transforms into happiness. When people are happy, they bring positive light into this world and that is what we need.

My angels have also told me that those of us who have experienced miracles are given gifts. We are healers. In the beginning, a few people started to reach out to me and I realized that my stories and abilities could help them. I originally thought it was just the old me, offering compassion and a few kind words.

I realized at some point, though, that God was allowing me to heal people! I was transformed into a wonderful conduit of His healing energy and I was excited! I don't completely understand how it works or if it will always work but I will always do my best. If it is to be, He will make sure that it happens. I have been told that this healing energy can manifest in many forms; including the power of a gentle touch, a few prayerful thoughts and even in a few simple words. I have also learned that anyone can be a healer if they so desire! And the world certainly needs more healers!

So, with the power of my loving intent and these written words, I am reaching out to offer each and every one of you a blessing. My angels have told me that everyone that has shown interest in my story will receive one; even those that have simply read this book! They have also told me that those who actually request assistance from the divine world will receive the most blessings. Some will even experience complete healing!

So, I encourage each of you to reach out to that wonderful heavenly world and believe that anything is possible. Angels and other divine beings are available for each and every one of us and will communicate, guide and heal us through God. All you have to do is ask.

Epilogue

Angel Talk

During the first year after my physical healing I continued to pray and found myself inspired on many different levels. Spiritually, my angels taught me to let go of the past, forgive others and forgive myself. Physically, they encouraged me to begin a reasonable exercise program and showed me how to work it into my daily routine. They also taught me about opportunities that would not only fulfill my financial needs but would provide a sense of personal satisfaction and accomplishment.

I was inspired to begin writing, taking photographs, and to form my own company, which I appropriately called "Divine Guidance"! I also set up a page on a popular social networking site so I could share important angel messages and other valuable information with others. That page is now called "Angel Talk" so others will understand where the messages are coming from.

My angels also showed me various other ways of producing income, one of which was through buying a small jewelry shop! Amazingly enough, I have been able to generate enough money to pay my bills since I opened the door! It has also served as a wonderful platform for me to share my story!

They also guided me into making time every day to do "Angel Talk" where I sit and do a simple meditation and they communicate the important stuff. This is where the book idea came in! Other significant messages come through when I'm gardening, riding my bike, listening to music or just relaxing. Hmmm, do I see a common thread? Angels communicate best when we are doing what we are supposed to be doing; meditating, relaxing, getting in touch with nature.

I continue to receive these lessons and daily guidance from my angels and am encouraged to share what I have learned with others. They also want me to teach about their role in our lives. It is amazing to know that we have helpers just waiting to assist us with every aspect of our lives.

As of now, I can teach about them through "Angel Talk" readings and classes. During my readings, I deliver personal information that a client needs to know to be healthy and happy. This includes providing direction and tools to allow for emotional, physical and spiritual healing.

My basic "Angel Talk" class involves instructions on how to communicate with these amazing beings and how to interpret their messages. I will soon be writing "Guidebook to Angel Talk" in the very near future for those unable to attend my classes! My angels are also going to help me with additional books so keep an eye out! We have come up with several ideas already!

Each and every one of us has an innate ability to understand messages that the angels are trying to send us. They are here for everyone and will guide us if we slow down long enough to listen. If you'd prefer to ask God, Jesus or another heavenly being directly for guidance, then go ahead and do so. It is a personal choice and the techniques are the same. Someone will deliver your messages; just pay attention so that you don't miss them!

For me, angelic communication is a way of life. I receive audible guidance and messages continuously (as in 24/7). While working on this book, a very important message came through for my readers so I'll pass it on to you!

"If you do your part by living your lives like God intended for you to do, He will provide everything that you need to live a happy, fulfilling and prosperous life. In order to achieve this, though, you must follow several principles. You should be kind and compassionate towards others; offer love and forgiveness to everyone (including yourself); be charitable and morally upstanding; nurture your intellectual, physical and spiritual self; and have faith in God. By following the tenets above, amazing things will begin to happen in your life! You will be blessed with physical and emotional healings, bestowed with spiritual enlightenment; and opportunities for financial growth will shower upon you like raindrops! These blessings will be delivered by heavenly beings, including our beloved Jesus!"

As a side note to the above message, always remember that God knows everything so make sure that you "walk the walk!"

Appendix A

Legend of Chimayo

El Santuario de Chimayo is a small chapel located in the Sangre de Cristo Mountains of Chimayo, New Mexico. It is widely known as the Lourdes of America due to all of the miraculous healings that are reported to have occurred there.

Upon doing a little research, I found that there are many legends about the history of the area. Of the many stories that I have read, though, what strikes me the most is that they all have the same theme. There is something very extraordinary going on there.

It is reported that Native Americans inhabited the area as far back as the 12th century, long before the Spaniards were there. They believed that they shared their land with supernatural beings and that the hills in the area were sacred. They also believed that the hot springs and dirt had curative powers.

It is also believed that a Guatemalan priest known as the Father from Esquipulas was one of the first settlers to the area. He supposedly brought with him a very large crucifix and preached to the Indians of the area. Eventually, he was killed by the Indians and was buried near Chimayo along with the crucifix.

The crucifix subsequently resurfaced and is now one of the focal points in the chapel. How it surfaced adds to the mystery and intrigue of this place. There are several differing variations as to how it was discovered. Some stories are a result of oral traditions and others have been reconstructed from historical documents. Any way you look at it, all of the stories are interesting.

In one of the accounts, it is believed that the cross and the body of the priest were uncovered in 1810 after the Santa Cruz River flooded. Locals in the area recognized him and began to associate the cross with the priest's origins in Esquipulas, Guatemala. After that, the crucifix was referred to as Our Lord of Esquipulas. It is unclear from this version as to what happened to the cross after it was found.

Another story claims that Don Bernardo Abeyta, a local settler, was performing penances in the area during Holy Week. and noticed a strange white light emanating from a nearby hillside. He went to investigate and began digging in the dirt with his bare hands. He found the large crucifix, which he associated with Our Lord of Esquipulas.

A variation of this story claims that Abeyta received a vision while working his land. He was directed to dig underneath his plow and subsequently discovered the cross. He may have even been sick and received a healing from the dirt.

After the discovery, Abeyta contacted the local priest, who, along with parishioners, took the crucifix back to their church in Santa Cruz. The next morning, the crucifix disappeared from the church and was found at its original location. For the second time, the crucifix was ceremoniously transported to Santa Cruz. It was again placed in the niche of the main altar. The following morning, it mysteriously disappeared and was found back on the hillside. After the third disappearance, it was generally understood that the cross was not supposed to be moved. A chapel was then built at the site where the crucifix was first discovered. Miraculous healings were soon reported and by 1816, the original chapel had to be replaced by the current larger one.

As I did the research for this information, I realized a few things. Just like all legends, the facts tend to change over the years. It is easy to confuse them while retelling an interesting story. Many also tend to embellish things a bit for what is known as dramatic effect. It is not that there is deceit involved, sometimes the additions help the story make a better point.

Personally, I don't believe it is all that important to know what the facts are about Chimayo. The variations in the story add to the intrigue and mystery about what really happened. It sparks our curiosity and our desire to learn more. Regardless of what version about Chimayo is correct, the message is all the same. People are claiming miracles from this wonderful place and this inspires others to believe in them as well. It is all about the power in faith.

CPSIA information can be obtained
at www.ICGtesting.com
Printed in the USA
FSOW01n0118300715
9385FS